D1025698

Colin White & Laurie Boucke

The UnDutchables

an observation of the netherlands: its culture and its inhabitants

Artwork:
Gerald Fried, Joe Cramer, Huug Schipper/Studio Tint

Photography:
Laurie Boucke, Colin White

WHITE BOUCKE PUBLISHING

Lafayette, Colorado

First Published December 1989
ISBN 0-9625006-0-7
Reprinted June 1990.

Second Edition February 1991
ISBN 0-9625006-1-5
Reprinted April 1991, October 1991, March 1992, May 1992.

Third Edition February 1993
ISBN 0-9625006-3-1
Reprinted September 1993, February 1994, December 1994,
March 1995, August 1995 (with updates), December 1995,
March 1996, June 1996, November 1996, March 1997.

ISBN: 0-9625006-3-1

Library of Congress Catalog Card Number: 93-233338

Printed in USA

WHITE
BOUCKE
PUBLISHING
PO BOX 400, LAFAYETTE, CO 80026, USA

preface

VERSION 3.1 -- the third edition (updated) . . .

This latest version of *The UnDutchables* has been updated to incorporate recent events and changes, including the 1995 floods.

The book presents an impressionistic view of a certain side of the Dutch as it is often perceived by visitors to Holland. It has brought laughter and joy to thousands of readers, and that is one of its primary objectives.

This is not a dry, scholarly work. It is not possible to cover every province, town, custom and aspect of life in such a short work -- such information is available elsewhere. We have avoided such an approach as it would have stifled the character of the book. Some readers may resent what they perceive to be a stereotypic image, but all people form such images (to some extent) when they travel or reside abroad. Fortunately, most readers have been able to appreciate the humour and exaggeration without feeling offended.

Although much of the book clearly concerns contemporary Dutch life, certain national traits have been around for centuries. These have been commented upon in works dating back to the 1600's. We believe the Dutch will still be renowned for certain classic characteristics for many generations to come.

Similarly, the book is biased towards the urban environment. However, in traveling through the countryside, one finds many of the same things, perhaps in a more peaceful setting and at a slower pace, but fundamentally the same traits: cosy homes; coffee rituals; guilder worshipping; moralizing; criticizing; obsession with weather; commercial cunning; and so forth.

In closing this Preface, we would like to thank all those who have provided ideas, suggestions and anecdotes, with special mention to *Brendan Bartram, Eva Goetschel, Anton van Hooff, Jackie Lubeck, Nijgh & Van Ditmar, Radio Nederland Wereldomroep, Wim Stortenbeek, Jaap Vossestein* and *Walter Wynbelt*.

Colin White & Laurie Boucke
August 1995

foreword

The fact that a third edition of The UnDutchables makes its appearance within three years after the introduction of the first edition proves that the book is a success in the wide circle of its readers.

The authors, both of Anglo-Saxon origin, have lived a good many years in the Netherlands and, as many foreigners, have been both surprised and astounded by our queer habits and customs, to such an extent that they have laid their impressions down in this monograph.

In this book, the Dutch find themselves confronted with a kind of mirror, and it hardly calls for surprise that a few of my fellow countrymen have reacted in a negative way to what they experience as "undue criticism." Nevertheless, most of the contents of the book are based on sound observations and the general tenor is never far away from the truth, although sometimes described in a somewhat caricaturistic way.

This third edition has been improved in a good many ways. The drawings have been refined, as compared with former editions, and quite a few photographs have been added. A number of new subjects has been brought in for description such as national dishes. The authors are keen observers: Did any *"cloggy"* ever realize that his way of peeling fruit is quite different from that of foreigners?

In a new section on the relationship between wealth and the hidden Dutch conscience, the authors have not hesitated to study the current literature on this subject and worked themselves through the bulky volume of Simon Schama on this particular aspect of the Dutch attitude.

But not all additions in the third edition are dead serious: The reader will experience a lot of fun in the description of a Dutch birthday party, and the average Dutchman will all of a sudden realize how tedious and narrow-minded some of his customs are!

The addiction to coffee is aptly illustrated (and with a lot of humour) in the description of the result of one of our famous coffee contests, and the final judgments on some of these cups are really laughter-raising.

The chapter on children's upbringing might come as a bit of a shock to the Dutch, but isn't it really time to realize that we do overspoil the little brats, far more than in most other countries? This chapter in former editions has been misinterpreted by some people as *"hate against children"* on the part of the authors, but I think that it is love and affection for children which moved the authors to lay down their impression of what they see as doing harm to our offspring, rather than trying to give them the benefit of a well-balanced upbringing.

A list of intrinsic idioms is developed further in this edition and might be particularly useful for people of Anglo-Saxon origin who would have to live in the Netherlands for a couple of years. Finally, an index has been added and comes in handy for quickly glancing through a subject in which one might have particular interest.

A last word about the writers themselves: Having moved to the USA a few years ago, the authors find it difficult to keep abreast of all the turbulent events in our ever-changing Dutch society. They are avid readers of some of our Dutch newspapers and magazines and are in perpetual touch with a number of Dutch friends, asking them continuously for closer explanations on all kinds of subjects in our daily press. I feel privileged to belong to this group of advisors and not only hope, but certainly expect this further elaborated and enriched version of former editions to be as successful as its predecessors.

To my fellow countrymen I should like to say: *Try not to be hurt by remarks on a pattern of behaviour that seems to be so completely normal to us, but in fact is sometimes quite out of this world when seen through foreign eyes!*

Dr . W. Stortenbeek
Apeldoorn, Holland
September 1992

contents

1. INTRODUCTION (the way the text books sell it)

There 1

Them 2

2. GETTING ACQUAINTED

There 5

Them 6

3. PUBLIC TRANSPORT

Tickets 12

What to Take 16

Waiting for Public Transport 17

On-board Activities 18

Behaviour 19
Taxis 21

4. **A DUTCH HOME**
Urban Architecture 24
Stairs 27
Furnishings 28
Window Pains 28
The Toilet 30
The Kitchen 33
House Pets 34
Houseboats 34

5. **A GROWING CONCERN**
Flower Power 37
Guilder Builder 39
Ground Rules 42
Timber Talk 43
Udder Things 45

6. **CHILDREN**
Kid Kreation 48
Raising Modern Dutches and Dutchesses 49
Typical Behaviour Patterns 50
Matériel 52
Holland's Future 54

7. **CINEMA**
Behaviour 58
Intermission 58
Subtitles 59
A Bad Case of the Clap 60
A Concert Next Time? 60

8. **MONEY (on gulden pond)**
Bargain Hunting 63
Street Markets 64
Second-hand Transactions 65

Shelling Out for Fuel. 66
Fines 66
Banks. 68
A Sporting Chance? 69
The Baud Bunch. 70
At Times of Sadness 72
Why? 73

9. UITKERING (the dutch work ethic)

The System I – Methodology 76
Work Attitude 77
Dismissal – Failure or Success? 78
Subsidies 79
Time-off 81
The System II – Consequences. 82

10. MET WIE? (identification & telephone habits)

Official Documents. 83
Place and Date. 84
I.D.-ology (proof of identification). 84
Introductions. 86
Telephone Manners 86

11. THE NATIONAL PASSION

Discussion and Debate 92
Complain, Protest, Object, Appeal 93
Causes 95
'The Dutch Way' 98
The House of Her. 99
Military Service 103

12. RULES FOR SHOPPING

General. 108
In Supermarkets. 108
Statiegeld and Borgsom 110
Shopping for Clothes 111
At Street and Flea Markets 112

13. DRIVING

Freewheeling Ways 113
Road Rights. 115
Traffic Jams 116
Getting Your Licence 117

14. ON DUTCH CUSTOMS

Non-racist Nation. 121
Manners Maketh Man. 124
Camping. 125
Sign Language. 127
On Marriage 127
The Coffee Cult. 129
The Other Cult. 133
The Birthday Party 135
Other Festive Occasions 136

15. BIKES, DIKES, FLAGS & FAGS

Bikes 140
Dikes 144
Flags I – Patriot(ic) Games. 145
Flags II – Regal Rubbish (and its disposal) . . . 148
Fags (and Fagettes) 152

16. THE DUTCH LANGUAGE

Throat Disease (pronunciation). 157
Grammar. 158
Trend Setters. 159
Spelling Corruptions 159
Intrinsic Idioms 160

17. FOOD FOR THOUGHT (culinary character)

Some Traditional Dishes 163
Midday Morsels 165
Restaurants. 168
Snack Bars 169
Tip(ple)ing. 170

Dutch Sushi. 172
Dutch Rusk 172
Dropjes. 174
Coveted Cookies 176
... and Dirty Dishes 176
Bottom of the Bottle. 177

18. SEX 'N DRUGS AND ROCK 'N ROLL
Sex as an Activity 180
Sex as an Industry 182
Drugs I – Still Smokin' 185
Drugs II – The Hard Line 187
Crime and Punishment 188
Rock 'n Roll, etc. 189

19. THE FLYING DUTCHMAN (export models)
The World According to Jaap 194
The Right Stuff 197
Colonial Cloggies 204
The Pretorian Disgard 209
Down-Under Dutch. 212
New World Netherlanders 220

20. ANOTHER BRICK IN THE WAAL
Dike-otomy of a Disaster. 227
Hans Verdrinker. 229

APPENDICES
A View of the Dutch through the
English Language. 243
A Chosen Selection of Dutch/
English Homonyms. 247
In Case You Don't Believe Us 251

INDEX

Holland occupies less than one percent of the
earth's surface . . . Its airline covers the rest.
KLM Royal Dutch Airlines
advertisement, 1993

chapter 1

INTRODUCTION

the way the text books sell it

There

A country (often called Holland) in western Europe bor-
dering on the North Sea, with Belgium on its southern
frontier and West Germany on its eastern flank; official
language, Dutch; capital, Amsterdam; seat of government,
The Hague; population (1995), 15.7 million.

Them

The area was occupied by Celts and Frisians who came under Roman rule from the 1st century BC until the 4th century AD and was then overrun by German tribes, with the Franks establishing an ascendancy during the 5th-8th centuries. During the Middle Ages it was divided between numerous principalities. The northern (Dutch) part (part of the Habsburg Empire) revolted in the 16th century against Spanish attempts to crush the Protestant faith and won independence in a series of wars lasting into the 17th century, becoming a Protestant republic. The southern part was absorbed into the Spanish Habsburgs and then in 1713 into the Austrian Habsburgs. Prior to wars with England and France, the country enjoyed great prosperity and became a centre of art and scholarship as well as a leading maritime power, building up a vast commercial empire in the East Indies, South Africa and Brazil. In the 18th century it sharply declined as a European power. In 1814 north and south were united, but the south revolted in 1830 and became an independent kingdom (Belgium) in 1839. Luxembourg gained its independence in 1867. The Dutch managed to maintain their neutrality in World War I, but were occupied by Germany in World War II. The post-war period has seen the country turn away from its traditional dependence on agriculture, although agriculture is still an important part of the economy. In 1960, large quantities of natural gas were discovered in the north; the ensuing wealth helped the Dutch mold their country into a "super" welfare state and emerge as a key figure in the new-look United Europe. In 1994, a liberal/socialist/environmentalist government took office, opening the dikes even further to a flood of progressive pampering.

NOTE...... The authors acknowledge *"The Oxford Reference Dictionary,"* 1986, for much of the information contained in this chapter.

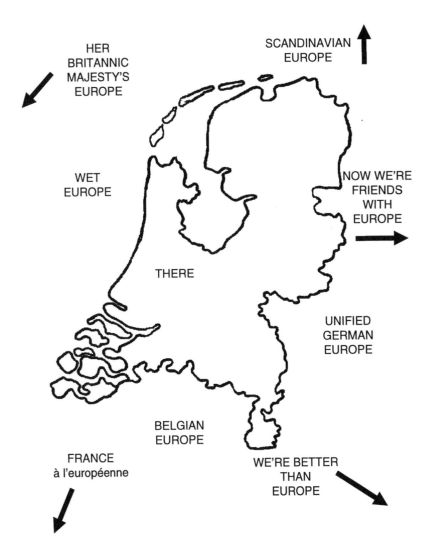

HER
BRITANNIC
MAJESTY'S
EUROPE

SCANDINAVIAN
EUROPE

WET
EUROPE

NOW WE'RE
FRIENDS
WITH
EUROPE

THERE

UNIFIED
GERMAN
EUROPE

BELGIAN
EUROPE

FRANCE
à l'européenne

WE'RE BETTER
THAN
EUROPE

Most people only get to visit great works of
art . . . The Dutch get to live in one.
KLM Royal Dutch Airlines
advertisement, 1988

chapter 2

GETTING
ACQUAINTED

There

Do not be surprised if one of your first impressions is of
being in doll-house country. Everything is small, crowded
and cramped: houses, streets, shops, supermarkets, parks,
woods, cars, etc. Holland is the third most densely
populated country in the world (after Bangladesh and
South Korea), and its inhabitants have mastered the art of
using the centimetre to its fullest.

This ability and talent has arisen, of course, from the fact that much of the country consists of land reclaimed from the sea. And the reclaiming continues even today.

On an international flight, when the pilot announces that you are flying over Holland, don't blink! You'll miss it -- it's that small. You can, in fact, cross the whole nation by car in three hours.

For those of you arriving by plane from distant lands, a word of advice. Having entered the country and adjusted to the barometric pressure prevalent below sea-level (jet-lag withstanding), you'll undoubtedly want to view the wind-mills, tulips, cheese markets and canals. Water and horizontal hills abound. So do sex shops. And, yes, you'll see your share of wooden shoes and Frisian cows. These tourist attractions can be exhausted within a day or two.

If you expect to find delicious national food or the exotic, forget it. If you like wide, open spaces or a little solitude in nature, this is not the country for you. There are no large forests or wide expanses of land. When walking in the woods, dunes or on the beach, you have the feeling that millions have trod wherever you place your feet. They have. Can this be the stuff that inspired Rembrandt and Van Gogh?

Them

The inhabitants of this small strip of ex-seabed are not lacking in self-esteem, as reflected in literary titles such as *"And the Dutch created the Netherlands" (En de Neder-landers Schiepen hun Eigen Land)* or *"Holland -- The New Atlantis Risen."* They are bursting with dikes, freedom, liberalism, independence, equality and political beliefs

(Holland boasts at least 29 parties), as will be demonstrated in the ensuing chapters.

The Dutch appear a friendly lot: kind, polite and helpful to tourists. They love to talk about their country and to provide any directions or information you may require. Their fascination with things foreign – products, attitudes, ideas, customs, languages, etc. – is impressive and flattering. The Dutch reputation for tolerance is all too apparent to the foreign visitor. But do not let this image fool you – it changes drastically if you stay long enough to be regarded as PART OF THE SCENE.

The longer you stay, the deeper you sink into it. The dark cloud of disapproval descends as your comrades of the Lowlands constantly criticize what they consider to be unfavourable situations beyond their borders. There is no relief from this moralizing, despite the fact that similar or even worse situations often exist within their own kingdom. Do not take the onslaught personally. You will soon discover that the Dutch reprimand is not reserved for foreigners alone. The natives thrive on shaking their fingers at and scolding each other.

They also seem to be caught up in a cycle of endless envy. They cannot free themselves from feelings such as, "If you are sitting, then I should be sitting, too!" They are extremely jealous of each another's possessions and keep a constantly updated mental inventory of what their neighbours, relatives and colleagues have. But they are also a very giving people when it comes to charities and other causes. They are world famous for their universal humanitarianism, and exercising this particular type of generosity gives them much peace of mind.

They always speak their mind and ask what most foreigners consider to be probing questions about one's personal life. Their directness gives many the impression that they are rude and crude – attributes they prefer to call *"openness."* You can put it to the test by discussing intimate and shocking topics with them that you would never dare speak about with any other nationality. What may strike you as being blatantly blunt topics and comments are no more embarrassing or unusual to the Dutch than discussing the weather.

This frankness is linked to their reputation for being opinionated and obstinate. When they believe in something, they will stubbornly adhere to their principles through thick and thin, unless and until they are ready to change their mind of their own accord. When necessary, they adopt and maintain a firm national resolve to "never again" let certain tragedies recur.

Over the centuries, they have developed and refined a sort of sand psychology which manifests itself in many walks of life. Since most of the country is built on sand, the use of lego-roads is widespread. Streets are paved with bricks which are merely pounded into place. The brick surface has no graded foundation layers. This construction method, combined with the Northern European climate, guarantees maximum inconvenience for motorists, cyclists and pedestrians: dips in the roads, sinking tramlines and a multitude of closed roads while re-flattening/re-laying operations are in progress.

The Dutch proudly defend the character of their roads. Workmen need only lift up the requisite amount of bricks to reach the work area. One wonders if they would need to lift up any bricks at all if they constructed the roads properly in the first place.

A *cloggy's* prize possession is The Bicycle. It may be a 15-speed, ultra-light, racing model or a rusty old third-generation job, honourably handed down through the family. Hence the country is infested with the contraptions.

The Dutch are masters of innovation, although some visitors may never identify or appreciate the results. Innovation and experimentation are constantly applied to a revolving process of refinement of social issues, agriculture and industry, and as urban and rural development. Sometimes the experiments are a success; sometimes they fail. Either way, new experiments will replace the gains or losses sooner or later.

Hollanders enjoy one of the highest standards of living and rank among the leaders of longevity. Their quality of life is excellent, although this fact is often disguised by constant complaining about the same.

They are supreme masters of things connected with water: bridges, dikes, canals, rain, etc. They have had to constantly defend their sand against natural elements with an elaborate survival system, as they WILL NOT HESITATE to tell you. This defence has been far more successful than that employed against many a human foe, as they will NEGLECT to tell you.

They have been a seafaring people for centuries on end. Along with this comes their love of travel, foreign cultures and bartering. There is nothing more exciting or satisfying for a Dutch person than to make a good deal. They have all the patience and time one can imagine if it means earning or saving a guilder or two. They are also world trade experts, ranking first place (worldwide) in tonnage at Rotterdam (with Hong Kong second) and first place in dairy and poultry export, while their agricultural export value ranks second in the world. Rotterdam also boasts of being the world's first fully automated container port.

Perhaps it's the age-old connection between water and cleansing/purification that drives them to it. Many of them are pathologically obsessed with a form of cleanliness which logically has little connection with practical hygiene. This is especially true of the older generation. It seems the older they grow, the cleaner everything must be.

It should be noted that the older generation appears to be exempt from much of what follows in this book. Although they are still in full possession of their Dutchness, it does not manifest itself as intensely as before. Perhaps after 60+ years, they are finally prepared to hand the baton to their heirs. Or it may be that most of the elderly have suffered at least one period of extreme hardship, such as having lived under the occupation of a genocide-obsessed *Drittes Reich* (Third Reich), which permits them to . . .

---

view the world with a more worldly view.

---

*Holland is not a bad place to eye up all
sorts of mass transit electric rail
traction developments.*
Paul J. Goldsack,
Mass Transit, 1985

chapter 3

PUBLIC
TRANSPORT

In addition to the national train service, Holland, like most countries, utilizes regional bus companies to provide for local public transport. Larger urban areas also have tram systems, and Amsterdam and Rotterdam have a metro train service. The public transport system is excellent. It is efficient, modern and comfortable. There are also ample taxis which can be expensive, especially over longer distances. All other forms of public transport are reasonably priced, if you know the rules of the game. If you don't, look forward to a frustrating and expensive experience.

Tickets

The physical size of Holland allows the bus companies to merge their ideas so that the whole country is divided into numbered travel zones. Tickets are valid for a quantity of travel zones and for a specific time, based on the number of zones crossed. You are free to travel anywhere within the defined multi-zone boundary for that period of time.

So far it seems simple. To travel from, say, Hilversum to Loosdrecht by bus, you must purchase a ticket for the requisite number of zones. Sorry, but it's not quite as simple as that. Disregarding season tickets, you have two options:

1. Purchase a blank ticket beforehand from a designated shop (post office, tobacconist, train station, etc.). The national strip ticket *(strippenkaart)* is divided into a number of lateral strips. A strip ticket can be used on any bus, tram or metro in the country. All you need to do is correctly stamp it in one of the yellow boxes provided, or ask the driver to do so. Knowing how to stamp the ticket correctly is too complex to explain in this account. In order to take your mind off the traumas of planning the next journey, some strip tickets carry a convenient word puzzle on the reverse.

2. Purchase a ticket on board. This is a less desirable method to use, since this ticket is considerably more expensive per zone than one purchased in a shop.

The national train service (*Nederlandse Spoorwegen*) has a simpler system whereby you purchase a travel ticket at

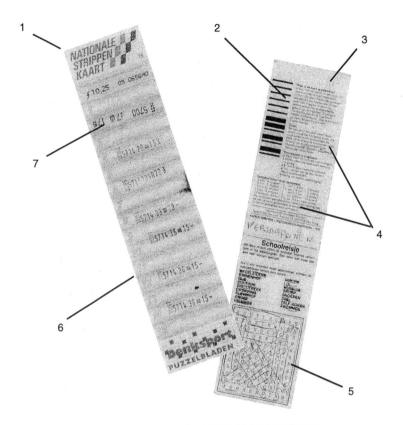

1. USE CORNERS AS A TOOTHPICK OR TO CLEAN BENEATH
    THE FINGERNAILS.
2. TRY TO READ OR DECIPHER THE BARCODE.
3. USE EMPTY AREAS TO STORE TELEPHONE NUMBERS, ETC.
4. ATTEMPT TO UNDERSTAND THE TICKET CONDITIONS AND ZONE TIMES.
5. COMPLETE THE PUZZLE. IF NECESSARY, ASK TO USE ANOTHER
    PASSENGER'S TICKET.
6. COVER ZONE STRIPS WITH "MAGIC" TAPE. LATER, WHEN TICKET IS FULLY
    USED, ERASE STAMPS OR REPLACE TAPE. IN THIS WAY, THE TICKET
    CAN BE USED MANY TIMES.
7. FOLD EACH STRIP LIMIT LINE FORWARDS, THEN BACKWARDS. THIS
    MAKES IT ALMOST IMPOSSIBLE TO INSERT INTO A TICKET STAMPING
    MACHINE. IT CAUSES GREAT ENJOYMENT TRYING TO DO SO AND
    ANNOYS THOSE WAITING TO STAMP THEIRS.

OTHER USES FOR COMPLETE TICKETS –
    AS A FAN (ON HOT DAYS), AS A BOOKMARK, AS A POINTING DEVICE.

The strip ticket and its hidden pleasures

the point of departure for the journey. To take the boredom out of this mundane task, a range of ticket categories has been introduced which will defy the most adept financial wizard. In fact, the matter has become so complex that *Nederlandse Spoorwegen* has issued a travel/price guide on diskettes (DOS and Windows *platforms*) to give the potential traveller a fighting chance at getting a fair deal on the journey price. To use the *Reisplanner* program, you enter the starting point and destination and the date and time of travel, and it will display your ticket options -- with prices. Thus if you are touring the country, a laptop computer will serve you well as an addition to the other items you will need. (See "What to Take," this chapter.) On a grander scale, computerized "journey planners" using touch screens to access nationwide public transport databases are being installed at bus and railway stations -- all for a country where you can travel the full perimeter in 24 hours.

```
amsterdam cs -> (T) zwolle              7:00 vertrek  17 februari 1992
                     [ Prijzen geldig vanaf 1 april 1991 ]
 Tariefafstand : 111 km.

                         2e Klas    2e Klas    1e Klas    1e Klas
                                    Reductie              Reductie

    Enkele reis        f   23,50  f   14,00  f   35,25  f   21,00
    Dagretour              38,50      23,00      57,75      34,50

  * Avondretour                        14,00                21,00
  * Weekendretour                      23,00                34,50

    5-Retourkaart         182,50     109,00     274,00     163,50
    Weektrajectkaart      118,00      70,00     178,00     106,00
    Maandtrajectkaart     445,00     267,00     667,00     400,00
    Jaartrajectkaart     3420,00               4830,00

    Jeugdmaandkaart       356,00     213,00

  * Alleen in combinatie met NS reductiekaart.
```

F1-Heen F2-Terug F3-Herhaal Andere toets-Oplossingen Ctrl_Home-Einde

A Reisplanner pricing guide

When you join the train-ticket queue, you will notice a curious sight. After purchasing a ticket, the average *cloggy* takes one side-step (usually to the left) and spends a few moments fiddling before departing with a satisfied look. Foreigners might think the side-step is part of the ticket purchasing process. Wrong. The *cloggies* (male or female) are merely organizing and taking an inventory of their coin purses, and putting their tickets into their handbags.

Until 1985, tickets were rarely inspected on urban transport. In 1985 it became apparent that the honour system had failed since the transport companies were losing a lot of money

Groups of inspectors were introduced. At first, the controllers frequently dressed in plain clothes. This uniform was soon eliminated by the democratic Dutch who complained that a *zwart* ("black," fare-evading) passenger should have a fair chance to escape. Now the controller-teams consist of groups of uniformed youngsters (in their teens or early 20's). A typical team consists of one or two females, one blond Dutchman and a combination of Turks, Surinamese and/or Negroes. These youngsters are often lenient with people who have not stamped their tickets properly.

However, do not be surprised to witness the youngsters frantically tackling a would-be escapee trying to get out of a metro train when it stops at a station. The controllers may find it necessary to grab the person in question. If he tries to escape from their grasp, the train will be delayed for the duration of the struggle on the platform.

Eventually the controllers will drag the escapee back into the metro train. The doors then close and the train proceeds as the escapee passionately protests, *"I haven't done anything wrong . . ."*

Still, there were too many *zwartrijders* for the *Nederlandse Spoorwegen* who, in retaliation, abandoned the possibility that any passengers had any form of honour. From the start of 1995, all passengers, platform spectators, pimps, passers-by, and pooches from poodles to pit-bulls had to pre-purchase a ticket. The public characteristically translated this outrage as *"cruel and unusual punishment"* and used its famed pacificity to engage in on-board fights and attacks on individual inspectors. *Nederlandse Spoorwegen*, not wishing to be derailed, responded by teaming inspectors, the cost of which has probably exceeded the losses attributed to *zwartrijders* in the first place.

What to Take

All nationalities have their habits and traits when it comes to public transport, especially on longer journeys. The Russians may take vodka or a chess set. Some nationalities will take their livestock to market on a bus. Instead of taking sheep, chickens and goats with them on public transport, the Dutch like to take their Bicycles, reading matter and at least one very large bunch of flowers for everyone to admire. You can buy a special ticket for your Bicycle. Reading matter and flowers go free of charge since:

- They bring so much joy to the passengers.
- They are an excellent conversation piece.

Finally, the Dutch love to take dogs on all forms of public transport. Dog tickets are on sale if the dog is too large to fit in your shopping bag or prefers to sit on its own seat.

Waiting for Public Transport

1. Whether you're waiting for the bus, tram, metro or train, form a compact mass with the others who are waiting, and do so as soon as the vehicle appears in the distance. When it arrives, block the doors so the exiting passengers cannot leave. Above all, do not move out of the way when the doors open and people attempt to get out, as this might speed things up. After all, you wouldn't want anyone to get ahead of you in the mob.

   If, however, you are a passenger waiting to exit, then you have the right to curse the stupid idiots blocking your way.

The proper way to do it

2. In rush hour, there will be enough of you to form
an additional blockade. Stand or slowly stroll so
as to prevent those who have managed to exit
from hurrying to the stairs or escalator, or to a
connecting bus or tram. In this "pinball" game,
you score points each time someone bumps into
you or is otherwise inconvenienced and frus-
trated by you.

On-board Activities

If you want to blend into the local colour, be sure to
passionately discuss the favourite topic of the country:
guilders.

It is compulsory for Dutch nationals to complain, whine
and express disapproval of subsidy levels, welfare benefits,
food prices and the economy in general. However, it is
highly inadvisable for non-Dutch to air negative views on
Dutch ways.

If the train is waiting at a stop and it is quiet in the
compartment, the mere rattling of a plastic bag is enough
to draw the attention of all those within earshot. They'll
immediately stop all present activities in order to try and
see what you're going to pull out of the bag (and probably
read whatever is written on the back of the bag).

Select your reading material to impress whoever happens to sit near you. It is obligatory that the person(s)
sitting near you spend a considerable part of the journey
studying your reading matter. Depending on their mood,
they may do this while holding up their newspaper as if
they are reading it, by casually glancing up from their book
or by just blatantly staring. It keeps them happy -- they are
studying free of charge.

These days, you see people carrying personal computer books with pride, even though they may have no interest in, and little understanding of, personal computers. Before the mid-1980's, there was much resistance to computer technology among the Dutch. Consequently, computer books were frowned upon; indeed, the average *cloggy* wouldn't be caught dead with a personal computer book. If you were one of the few who did choose to read on that taboo topic, you would have done so at your own risk and certainly only if the seats near you were empty.

If you choose to write instead of read, their curiosity will double.

Behaviour

Rules of behaviour on public transport are deeply ingrained in the Dutch. If you do not want to offend them, please observe the following:

1. If you are one of the first to enter the vehicle, spread your belongings out across the adjoining seat(s). Then stretch your legs out to block access to vacant seats. The rule is to sit in the aisle seat whenever the window seat is not occupied. If someone comes along looking for a place to sit, ignore him/her by looking away, reading a newspaper or pretending to be asleep.
   It is allowed to vacate seats for elderly/handicapped/pregnant people, but only to the extent that it remains the exception to the rule.

2. If the vehicle is full, you must stand inside the compartment where you are sure to block traffic when others want to pass through.

3. As the train approaches your destination, you must begin to fidget. If possible, stand up and fidget with your belongings.

4. Those in the back of the compartment must push, shove and/or stampede to the front of the car. (It is tempting to say "queue" since the way in which they stand vaguely resembles a queue; this is only because you must stand single file in the narrow compartment.)

Dutch law of motion:
"Exit time is inversely proportional to distance from door." In other words, those who sit nearest the door leave last. If you are in a hurry to get off the train, you must sit as far from the door as possible.

---

5. Upon arrival at glorious Amsterdam CS (Central Station), don't look anyone in the eye or you'll risk being hustled – for hashish, heroin, cocaine, a cheap hotel or botel (boat-hotel behind station), "sleep-in," petition signing, left-wing newspaper, right-wing newspaper, non-affiliated newspaper, shoe shine, joining in a demonstration or riot, recruiting squatters *(krakers)*, women's "lib" or gay "lib." In any case, staring at the floor/ground is good practice from the moment you exit the station and encounter the heaps of dog *shit* which decorate the streets of Amsterdam.

(Take no offence to our use of the word *shit*. The Dutch have adopted it as an everyday word in their vocabulary.)

Taxis

Dutch cities support an abundance of taxis. The cars are predominantly Mercedes-Benz and Opel vehicles. Their drivers are highly skilled in manœuvring through narrow side streets, ranks of pedestrians and other hazards. They are impervious to rules and masters of the spoken obscenity -- an instant introduction to local colour.

City taxis have their busiest moments at night. Taxis are dispatched to callers through a co-ordinating centre for local operations (*taxicentrale*). On a wet, cold winter's night, when public transport has stopped and you are stranded far from home, dial the *taxicentrale* and expect the following relief:

- A recorded message advising, *"Er zijn nog vijftien wachtenden voor U"* (15 calls ahead of you).
- Allow the recording to count down to one call ahead of you.
- When you are greeted by a human operator (usually with a curt *"TAXI!"*), tell him/her where you are and where you want to go.
- The operator recites the number of the local *centrale* for your district.
- Dial the local *centrale* and expect no answer.
- Redial the original *taxicentrale* number and start again.

There is no guarantee that a repeat effort will be more successful, but at least it stops you from falling asleep.

A new type of taxi was introduced in the **Randstad** (cities of western Holland) in 1990: the train taxi *(treintaxi)*. Travelers with a VALID train ticket can take a special taxi from any location in town to the train station (and, upon return, from the station to any location in town) for a mere HFl 6-. Don't forget, you must go to the station to buy your ticket, then return home to call the *treintaxi* to take you back to the station in order to cash in on the HFl 6- deal!

The instigation of this mode of transport produced prodigious protesting among "regular" taxi drivers since the *treintaxis* are subsidized by the Government. The solution to this upset was for the Government to announce that the *treintaxis* have not caused any losses to taxi companies, but have stimulated overall taxi travel to train stations.

Although we have attempted to confine the Dutch Drug Dilemma to one chapter of this book (see Chapter 18), it must be mentioned here that taxi companies in Eindhoven, The Hague, Rotterdam, Tilburg and other cities are legally permitted to deliver soft drugs (marijuana, hashish) door-to-door throughout surrounding districts using hash taxis *(hasjtaxis)*. The following conditions apply:

- No advertising to school children
- No sales to minors
- No nuisance or disturbance to local residents
- NO BUSINESS FOR PURE PROFIT-SEEKING.

As a reward for his/her services to the community, the Eindhoven *hasjtaxi* operator is subsidized to the tune of HFl 30,000 per year (1992). For more on the wonderful world of subsidies, see Chapter 9.

————————————

chapter 4

A DUTCH HOME

Ask a Dutch person about HOME and you will be told that it is *gezellig*, a word that they claim has no English equivalent. The dictionary translates it as *"cosy."* And, in this case, for *"cosy"* read *"cramped."*

The soul of the place is reflected through its living inhabitants -- plants, pets and people -- and the atmosphere *(sfeer)* is created by a widespread proliferation of inanimate objects. All these elements constitute *thuis* (home).

Urban Architecture

The classic Dutch look is the responsibility of 17th-century architects whose desire it was to maximize the impression of the height of a house. This, in conjunction with the then-as-now overcrowding in cities, led to the introduction of highly characteristic design elements (many of which survive to this day). The convention that the depth of a house should be greater than its width is a prime example, no doubt popularized by a housing tax which rated a dwelling on its breadth. The tall aspect of the famous canal buildings in Amsterdam is enhanced by the height of the windows being progressively reduced from bottom floor to top (but more about windows later). Given the *cloggy* passion to deny riches, prosperous locals generally insist on lesser external features:

---

*The narrowness of the nest negates
the wanton width of the wealthy.*

A typical old, urban house now provides four separate accommodation units, or *flats*. There are two front entrances to the building, commonly one for the ground floor owner and one for the elevated tenants. The very long and narrow staircase is found in the section leading to the upper floors. Inevitably, one or more Bicycles and a few thick, winter coats hang from the wall above the banister.

This efficient design provides:

- maximum inconvenience to those entering the building

- maximum disturbance to a resident hearing chattering, giggling, stomping locals enter or exit the building
- maximum inconvenience and disturbance to all concerned, by the uninitiated attempting self-disentanglement from The Bicycles (or trying to remove pedals, handlebars, etc., from an ear).

A curious architectural characteristic is located just below, or as part of the design of, the famous Dutch gable. A rusty old meat-hook hangs from a wooden or metal arm which extends from the front of the building. This is not a symbolic carry-over from the pacifist nation's barbarous past. The hook supports a pulley which allows large, heavy items of furniture, and other bulky possessions, to be hoisted up from ground level. The windows and their frames are constructed for easy removal, thus allowing the load enough space for entry into the house on any floor. Many a Dutchman fears the public disgrace suffered if the load is allowed to adopt a pendulous motion, entering the building through a neighbouring window.

Other notable exterior features (optional) include:

- a short metal tube, extending from the front wall at a 45-degree angle. This is, in fact, a flagpole holder used to support the national flag on patriotic holidays. The ground floor installations are also used as litter bins and cigarette butt containers by urban youths.
- the spy mirror *(spionnetje)*, mounted on or close to a window frame. It resembles a large auto-mobile "wing mirror" (probably stolen from a heavy goods vehicle) which older couples use to study street life, unobserved.

- a collection of old household junk, typically --
  gardening implements, toilet seat, wash basin
  etc., to add character to the abode.
- a series of tree trunks extending from the nearest
  kerb to the upper-front wall of the building. These
  wooden megaliths serve to provide neighbour-
  hood dogs with a natural toilet place, and to
  inconvenience pedestrians, cyclists and motorists
  alike. A secondary function is to stop the house
  from falling down.
- a human window cleaner, present and working
  at approximately four-weekly intervals --
  irrespective of weather, time-of-year or window
  conditions.

Subside-ized housing

Stairs

This marvelous invention – the Dutch staircase – is called a *trap*, and it is not uncommon to feel trapped when you climb the staircase. The *trap* will be steep and narrow, of meager depth, and will probably accommodate less than half your foot. In older houses, the staircase closely resembles a warped ladder.

Indeed, you must climb the stairs in the same way you climb a ladder, clinging precariously to the upper steps with your hands or to the banister (if there is one), with one dangerous difference: There is no room for your foot to extend over the steps for balance, as with a ladder. The lofty Dutch accept this ridiculous arrangement as a fact of life; it provides that essential exercise that other nations obtain from climbing hills.

Following the path of the stairs, a rope or heavy cord passes through a series of loops and runs from attic to ground floor, terminating in a series of indescribable knots attaching it to the street door latch. This high-tech device allows residents of all floors to open the street door to visitors without the necessity of negotiating the stairs, which would entail more exercise than is good for a *cloggy* (too much stair-exercise causes untold wear on shoes and floor/stair covering, resulting in premature replacement of both). Whatever you do, DO NOT use the rope as a banister when ascending the staircase. You will trip the door mechanism and will be obliged to return to the front door again to close it. Continued misuse will draw you into an almost perpetual-motion situation, cycling between climbing up the stairs, climbing down the stairs, closing the door, climbing up the stairs . . . .

Furnishings

The favourite furniture styles are either pseudo-futuristic (Scandinavian influence) or imitation classical/antique (German influence), including *stijl meubelen* (imitation Italian/Spanish renaissance pieces).

Rooms are literally cluttered with the stuff, adding to the sense of claustrophobia already caused by the:

* lack-of-size of the dwelling
* regulation Dutch colour scheme, consisting of insipid shades of curdled cream and excreta brown
* over-abundance of house plants (see Chapter 5).

One area must be dominated by a desk and cumbersome bookshelves. With these two items present, certain tax advantages can be gained. The content of the bookshelves displays the image the owner wants to project.

Window Pains

Windows are a focus for Dutch technology. In some respects, the character of a Dutch home is defined by the style of window installed. They are as much a conversation piece as the remainder of the place. The Dutch invest a large portion of their income in embellishing the interiors of their homes -- they need to show them off through large windows, yet are obliged to clutter the things up as much as possible to avoid accusations of egotism.

In contemporary homes, panes must be as large as possible and as technologically-advanced as possible.

When modernizing a house, strive to get the maximum number of "doubles" into your replacement windows:

- double size
- double glazing
- double opening
- double locking
- double impressive (style)
- double curtains (see below).

Be sure not to neglect your windows. They need plenty of cleaning (make sure your neighbours see this happening regularly) and protection (take out adequate window insurance). For the ultimate impression, have your windows professionally cleaned while it is raining.

Curtains are important in Dutch life. Almost every home has a double set of curtains: net curtains *(vitrage)* and heavier, full-length curtains. It is customary to leave the front-room curtains open day and night so everyone can look in and admire the possessions. Even the poorest of the Dutch get their hands on enough money to make their front room a showpiece, to give it their special *cloggy* atmosphere they feel is worth displaying to all passers-by. By true Dutch standards (see Chapter 8), the concept of paying for curtains by the metre and only enjoying a quarter of them is heresy. Upon further reflection, it seems highly likely that the "unused" width is in fact used to mask the emptiness from thieves, vagabonds and squatters *(krakers)* when the official dwellers are on vacation, or otherwise not *thuis*.

Some claim that the open-curtain convention stems from an old Calvinistic tradition indicating to passers-by that nothing "sinful" is happening. It is debatable in this current era of relaxed sexual preferences that such a pious principle presently persists.

Given that the average *cloggy* (having no control over the size of his/her windows) likes to have as many of the things as possible in order to afford maximum light into the dwelling, is it not paradoxical that much of this (free) light is blocked by the plethora of plants parked proximate the panes?

The Toilet

Nowhere is the sense of claustrophobia more pronounced than in the water-closet. The Dutch have taken the term literally and made that most private of rooms the size of a cupboard. Once you've managed to get inside the thing, you then face the problem of turning around to close the door and adjust your clothing. Before seating yourself, you face the dilemma of deciding whether you want your knees pressed tightly against the door or rammed under your chin. Any sense of relief on completion of your duties is counteracted by the realization that you must now find a way to manœuvre yourself up and out again.

By far the most distressing feature of the Dutch WC is the toilet itself. The bowl is uniquely shaped to include a plateau, well above the normal water level. Its purpose becomes obvious the first time you see (or use) one. Why the worldly, cultured Dutch have this sadistic desire to study the recent content of their stomach remains a mystery. Perhaps it is not the sight of the deposit fermenting on the "inspection shelf," but the personal aroma that emanates from the depths and lingers in the closet for hours after the offending substance has been launched on its final journey.

The flushing system is a technological wonder -- not so much a miracle of hydraulic genius, but more a case of *"find-the-flusher."* The Dutch seem to derive some form of sadistic pleasure in constructing the most bewildering launching mechanisms. Be prepared for any of the following:

- a button on the pipe leading to a high cistern
- a button at the front of a low cistern
- a button at the top of a low cistern
- a lever at the side
- a chain, rope or length of string
- a foot pedal
- a fish whose tail needs wagging
- a little boy whose tail needs wagging
- a linear motion, vertical action, flapper-valve actuating device (i.e. "knob") that needs pulling.

If you don't find one of these, check for a spring-loaded pipe extending from the bowl to the cistern. If you find one, pump it -- don't worry about your hand getting wet; it's all part of the game. If nothing works, return to your original location and complain about unhealthy people clogging up the works. Under normal circumstances, it's good sport; however, combined with the aforementioned aromatic horrors of the venue . . . enough said!

Whatever happens, don't pull the pipe extending from the front of a high cistern. This is an overflow pipe which will christen you with a large quantity of unblessed water for the duration of your occupancy. Even if it dripped on you earlier, please don't break it off now.

The toilet brush is another compulsory component. It is necessitated by the *"inspection shelf"* and is included in the whole spectrum of Dutch dwellings, both permanent and temporary. After using the toilet, a well-behaved guest

A Dutch toilet – what is missing?

will always clean the toilet bowl meticulously with the brush and chemical cleansers provided. From the poorest houseboat to the most exclusive and elegant hotel, the trusty toilet brush will always occupy a meaningful space in the chamber. It is an item accepted by all, mentioned by none, seen to be used by none, yet always wet.

Typical WC decor consists of a birthday calendar affixed to the door; the compulsory plant (heaven help it); reading matter; a can of ineffective air freshener; and an aged, corny sign or cartoon requesting men, pigs or bulls to lift the seat.

The Kitchen

Second place for the smallest-room award goes to the kitchen, if indeed a separate room exists for it. This room, or area, epitomizes the Dutch gift for efficient space utilization. In lower income homes, the whole area is cluttered with cooking pots, utensils, house plants and beer crates. An aging, white four-ring gas burner *(gasstel)* sits atop the refrigerator. In higher income homes, the whole area is bedecked with modern appliances (microwave oven, blender, juicer, food processor, etc.), house plants and beer crates. A stainless steel or brown four-ring *gasstel* sits proudly atop the smallest refrigerator.

Also prominently featured/displayed: a wide selection of exotic and ethnic herbs and spices (usually supported by wall charts and guide books), even if they never use them.

No Dutch kitchen would be complete without the coffee corner, a sacrosanct area displaying a drip-type coffee maker *(koffiezetapparaat)*, an array of jars and cans, an abundant supply of condensed milk *(koffiemelk)* and a collection of coffee cups, saucers and miscellaneous dwarf spoons. A pack of coffee filters is loosely pinned to the wall.

A small gas water heater *(geyser)* is usually mounted on the wall above the sink and provides hot water for the entire home. This configuration works well, provided only one hot water outlet is used at a time. If you take a shower and the water turns cold, it is probably because someone is filling a kettle in the kitchen.

House Pets

Favourite pets *(huisdieren)* include:

- cats (to catch mice)
- dogs (the smaller the abode, the larger the dog)
- fish (observation of which supposedly curbs violence)
- rabbits (for the children to cuddle)
- guinea pigs (for the rabbit(s) to cuddle)
- rats (to carry about town on owner's shoulder)
- exotic birds (to feel sorry for, locked in their cages).

A popular pet in country homes is the female goat, an ethnic symbol, to provide milk and cheese *(geitemelk, geite-kaas)*.

Houseboats

There are about 2,400 houseboats *(woonboten)* in Amsterdam alone. Houseboats became prevalent due to the extreme housing shortage at the end of World War II. They are ideal living places for those who find the average

Dutch house or *flat* too spacious. A houseboat is usually a shabby, converted canal barge which provides one or two cheap accommodation units. In general, canal boats have no rusty hook hanging from a gable; the *trap* is replaced by an unstable, narrow gangplank; the furnishings remain typical but fewer due to weight and structural limitations; the toilet cupboard is even smaller; and raw sewage drains directly into the canal in which the boat sits. Ventilation is generally poor, heating is by means of an oil-fired stove, and cooking is done on a butane or natural gas hob. All this makes the habitat a potential floating-bomb, and a houseboat home on a busy waterway adds a whole new meaning to the word HANGOVER.

Despite these minor inconveniences, it remains fashionable to reside in a houseboat. Perhaps this stems from nautical traditions. For many, it provides temporary escape from the surrounding brick and concrete. In any case, houseboat living is *"ethnic."* Even though most houseboats have been permanently retired from their conventional roles and never go anywhere, the owners tend to work incessantly to keep the propulsion system in pristine condition.

In Utrecht, the red-light district basically consists of a row of houseboats.

Houseboats I – The tourist view

Houseboats II – Home

A GROWING CONCERN

Flower Power

If you want to express thanks, gratitude or sympathy to a *cloggy*, give flowers (*bloemen*, sounds like "blue men"). If you would like to apologize or patch up a quarrel, resort to flowers. If you are invited to dinner at a Dutch home, be sure to arrive bearing flowers.

The Dutch offer flowers to each other on all sorts of occasions. Where some nationalities would send a greeting card or others would arrive with a gift or other token, the Dutch say it with flowers. A *cloggy* on a Bicycle with a large bunch of flowers is as symptomatic as a Frenchman carrying a long, thin loaf of bread.

Bunches of **bloemen** should ideally be carried petal-down, in order for the excess water (from their previous abode) to leak through the wrapping and run down your leg. Display the wrappered, soggy bundle in front of your hosts immediately upon arrival. They will transform before your eyes, as the essence of their *cloggy*-being is reflected in an expression of ephemeral euphoria on their faces. A flower-grooming and -rehabilitation ceremony will take place before you are invited to join them in their humble dwelling.

When you enter a Dutch home, be certain to take a machete with you to hack your way through the growth. The Dutch are proud of their obsession with plants and flowers to such a degree that the average living room resembles more a sub-tropical jungle than European living quarters.

When you finally find a place to sit, your gaze will undoubtedly fall upon additional vases of freshly cut flowers, prominently and strategically enshrined in highly visible locations. Further growth is nurtured just outside the windows, in both the front and back gardens where available or, in flats, on the window ledges or balconies. Given the diminished dimensions of a Dutch dwelling, the lovely leaves limit *Lebensraum* to ludicrous lengthlessness.

The image of horticultural Holland is the tantalizing tulip. Yet these tulips are less visible than the purely green goddesses in the domestic environment. Tulips are bought by the bunch, box and bushel, mainly for the benefit of others, or as a showpiece. As with so many other things, the tulip has been made a symbol of Dutchness . . . *of the Dutch, by the Dutch and for the non-Dutch.* Chapter19 explores this myth in greater detail.

Finding a place to sit

Guilder Builder

Needless to say, the flower industry thrives and therefore is a major source of revenue for the country. In parts
of the remaining countryside, flower fields resemble a
colourful patchwork quilt. Colder months and temperamental
genuses are no obstacle to the industry, thanks to green-
houses.

In towns and cities, flower shops, stalls and barrows are
abundant -- with prices to suit every pocket. Holland is the
largest exporter of cut flowers in the world. The flowers are
sold daily to vendors at a large flower auction in Aalsmeer.
The method used is the democratic "Dutch auction"

Flowers for the masses

(called "Chinese auction" by the Dutch) whereby the sellers bring the price down until someone makes the first bid.

Every ten years, a huge horticultural exhibition called the *Floriade* is held in Holland. This is a doubly-joyful occasion for Hollanders since they can bask in the excitement of two of their favourites: flowers and money. Or can they? The 1982 *Floriade* lost approx. HFl 9 million and despite this, it was considered an outstanding success. The reasoning (*clogic*) was that as the actual cost was HFl 36 million, they enjoyed a HFl 36-million show for only HFl 9 million. The 1992 spectacle boasted 2 million bulbs and 3.3 million visitors, but the outcome was still a negative profit. True to form, there immediately followed a simultaneous outpouring of feeling over:

- discontinuing the event, due to the magnitude of the successful losses.
- continuing the event (hopefully with less successful losses next time).

Amongst the latter clan, there is the characteristic in-fighting over who should be blessed with the prestige of paying host to the next *Floriade*, an event which many *cloggies* perceive as an eighth wonder of the modern world, reborn every decade.

A far more popular event (for the locals) is the *Bloemencorso*, an annual flower-float parade following a route through Aalsmeer, Amstelveen and Amsterdam, and which takes place in September (outside the normal European tourist season). It is a heart-warming moment to watch the local inhabitants delight in the colourful procession of flowered chariots as they pass by -- enthusiasm due mainly to the magnificent arrangements, but also because they are free to behold.

With such large amounts of finances flying, flower filchers have inevitably entered the arena -- big time. Organized crime has extracted much profit from the leaf-thief/petal-pusher circuits by stealing bunches of bouquets from flower cultivators and selling them anywhere and everywhere they can.

Horticultural hysteria is not the exclusive domain of petals. Anything green and growing is a certain money-spinner. Plants for home use and vegetables for export also command a large space in the fields and markets.

Acquiring a budding new family member is only the start. Plant paraphernalia (an ornate pot, special soil, humidity gauge, various types of plant foods, leaf shine, etc.) is purchased/upgraded without a great deal of thought for the purse. Whenever necessary, the household horticultural library expands with do-it-yourself books such as CARING FOR YOUR FAVOURITE HEVEA BRASILIENSIS and 1001 FIRST NAMES FOR YOUR NEW EUPHORBIA PULCHERRIMA.

It has yet to occur to the Dutch that all this growing of flowers and house plants wastes good soil that could otherwise be used to grow crops. The crops could be sent to the starving masses in Africa, a popular subject for more protests in Holland (see Chapter 11). The world now waits with bated breath for the Dutch to protest this abuse of their assets.

Ground Rules

One may think that incessant production of tulips, trees, tomatoes, turnips and 'taters would have rendered Dutch soil almost barren by now. Indeed not, for the regular application of cow crap *(mest)* and other fertilizing agents has kept their hallowed ground rich -- until recently, at least.

Fields are becoming polluted with the residue from the 95 tons of manure, annually donated by the 17 million cows and pigs (four-legged variety) that inhabit Holland. There's just too much *shit* there.

Eager to capitalize on the prospect of florins for free faeces, provincial authorities have set up "manure banks" for deposit and withdrawal of the stinky stuff. To guarantee success, bank charges are levied on all transactions, and the whole nonsense is government-subsidized. The latest word is that the *shit* banks are becoming a nationalized industry " . . . to promote efficient use of the surplus."

The whole issue of the *mest* mess commands more news space in Dutch dailies than the greenhouse effect (which some learned circles believe is partly caused by those same animals and their bovine belches).

Timber Talk

In keeping with their love of plant life, the Dutch have elevated the tree to almost "national symbol" status. Cities and villages provide generous budgets for the care and maintenance of trees. Each public tree is logged, numbered and carefully monitored. Tree doctors study, examine and perform surgery when necessary. If a tree is fortunate, has the right roots, is well-behaved, lives long and leaves itself well, it can be granted "monument" status. (Currently, more than 10,000 trunks have achieved this rank.) Tree foundations and *aktie* groups for trees do a blooming business. For instance, when a 130-year-old Leeuwarden sycamore tree was executed in order to make way for a theatre, a farewell ceremony was held at its last resting place. Flowers were laid in memory. (No doubt a memorial plaque for the tree will be erected in the theatre -- this tribute being constructed from choice wood from another victim of deciduous decapitation.)

The only form of tree-abuse tolerated is that executed by another over-protected species – *cloggy* kids (see Chapter 6), who happily maim, disfigure and mutilate the vegetation whilst experiencing freedom and union with nature.

Having said this, we now encounter a choice double standard of *clogism*. On the one hand, they export forest-loads of wooden shoes around the world, as a symbol of their country. On the other hand, they are fed up with the stereotype of the wooden shoe/windmill. A typical example

A Dutch dendro-paramedic

of this conflict manifested itself while we were originally preparing this book. A Dutch illustrator pleaded to know:

> *What kind of tune will the book whistle? Is it a book showing all Dutch people walking on wooden shoes, making porno pictures of their children for selling in the USA?*

In this ecologically-conscious, save-the-planet, celebrate-earth-day world, one wonders if the crime of *boom*icide in order to preserve windmill table lamps, footwear and foot-lockers is really valid. Holland is the second largest importer of tropical hardwood, after Japan (1991). Foreign forests are apparently less sacred than the Dutch variety, as the Netherlands Government has decreed that there should be no restrictions on the importation of wonderful wood from Latin lands.

Udder Things

Slightly out of place in this chapter, but important never-theless, is the subject of cows. Apart from their importance in emitting excrement (as discussed earlier), *cloggy* cows provide the main ingredient for Dutch dairy produce. With-out cows, there would be no famous football-cheeses, no discus-cheeses, no cream for their unique apple pies, no condensed milk for their coffee and no butter for their imitation sandwiches (see Chapters 11 and 17 for more on these delights), not to mention the effect on the export market. (Holland is the world's top exporter of dairy pro-ducts.) The place would simply not function well without cows.

So what can the *cloggies* do to improve the production of raw materials in this sphere? Revolutionize the milking process, of course.

One milking system, MIROS (Milking Robot System) uses ultrasound to locate a cow's teats:

1. On arrival at a milking stall, the animal is identified by a transponder worn around her neck.

2. A computer then checks when the last milking took place. If another milking session is due, the cow is retained in the stall.

3. A robot uses two ultrasound beams to locate the udder, then a rotating beam finds the individual teats.

4. After the teats have been found, a mechanical arm automatically attaches the milking machine to the teats.

One rival system relies on a computer which is programmed with each cow's vital statistics (teat positions; and udder location, size and shape) in order to attach the milking machine.

Overall, the new procedures fit in well with the Dutch way of doing things -- efficient and cost-effective, while making sure it is good for "Daisy." The cows seem to approve of the technique as they are FREE to enter the stall whenever they feel too full, and they show a measure of reluctance to leave when finished.

Now, if only some clever *cloggy* could adapt the system for use in urban areas to handle the output from dogs' rear ends !

chapter 6

CHILDREN

This chapter, despite its title, is not so much a comment on Dutch children themselves, but more a comment on their upbringing. As early as the 17th century, visitors to the land were both surprised and disconcerted by the over-indulgence that the Dutch displayed towards their young. They spoiled them then and have been refining the art ever since.

There are two basic ways to bring up *cloggy* kids:

- the common sense way by teaching them some manners and respect (mainly found in what's left of the countryside). Polite and well-behaved children are a delight for all concerned. As they do not attract much attention by their activities, they remain to a large extent invisible to outsiders.

- the classico-contemporary way as free, rude, spoiled, pampered gods. This category is very much in the majority and in this respect warrants further comment.

Kid Kreation

Holland is a great place to go through pregnancy and childbirth, as every Dutch parent will tell you. Midwives and physicians undergo thorough obstetric training and practice. Natural births are encouraged in most cases, and home is considered the best place to do it. Wherever the baby-falling *(bevalling)* takes place, a mystical atmosphere of cosiness and intimacy prevails between all present. Strangely, no fresh-cut flowers can attend. When the newborn finally arrives, it is treated with utmost respect and care – perhaps too much so.

During the first weeks of life, baby and its mother normally face an almost continuous stream of visitors: relatives, friends, nurses, advice-givers and well-wishers. The exhausted mother may well want nothing more than privacy and quiet with her newborn, but will find she must serve both infant and intruder – and not always in that order. The new parents (like all *cloggies*) love receiving gifts, but this makes them beholding to the interlopers, and the cycle continues. This constitutes one of baby's earliest extra-uterine lessons in the arts of independence, give-and-take and rebelliousness.

Raising Modern Dutches and Dutchesses

The golden rule is (and apparently always has been): Let them be free. Free to explore and experience whatever they please. Free to be "creative" (destructive), with little or no concern for anyone else, as long as they are not in serious danger. They must learn to be independent and rebellious AS YOUNG AS POSSIBLE.

In all this upbringing and education, children should not be kept on too tight a rein, but allowed to exercise their childishness, so that we do not burden their fragile nature with heavy things and sow untimely seed in the unprepared field of understanding.

Jan van Beverwijck, 1656

Speak to the little terrors in baby language and pamper them until they finish their childhood (around the age of 30).

Dutch families [in the 1600's] seem to have been much more reluctant than other contemporary cultures to relinquish their hold on the young.

S. Schama, 1987

In public, suggest discipline by giving loud instructions regarding behaviour that is permitted and that which is not. Angelface will immediately disobey by testing the instructions, whereupon cherub's activities are ignored.

DUTCH PARENTS BEWARE
Take a tip from nature: DO NOT overprotect your offspring. Tanja (a hippopotamus at Artis Zoo, Amsterdam) was found guilty of this when she smothered to death 5 of her 15 children, by hugging too hard, and starved another 5 by refusing to let them be fed by zookeepers. Tanja is now on birth control pills. Her mate, Joop, could not be reached for comment.

Typical Behaviour Patterns

If you visit a Dutch family, abandon all hope of being able to hold a reasonable conversation. A loud-mouthed child will inevitably:

- place itself between host(ess) and guest, where it will dance (sometimes on your feet) and chatter to get attention
- cuddle up to mother, stroke her face and hair or wriggle around in her lap, continuously asking stupid and unnecessary questions
- sit between you both, stare at you, and imitate your every facial expression and movement.

When the mother notices that you are about to leave because of her sweet child's behaviour, she will tell the child, in her sternest voice, to go away and "let mama talk." The child will ignore her until the command has been repeated at least three times. Within five minutes, the child will return. The mother will be delighted to have her free, little angel back (totally forgiven and welcome to continue its previous activities).

Other favourite antics for Dutch children are to yell, scream, fight, cry, run around the room, climb all over the furniture, slam doors, bump into you, etc., again making it impossible to converse.

This attitude of parent and child continues in public: waiting rooms, transport, schools, streets, restaurants and shops. Above all, beware of the cinema syndrome where the combined traits of the adult, adolescent and infant *cloggies* merge into three hours of sheer hell (see Chapter 7).

Two mothers board a metro train, along with five small children. One of the children places her dirty hands on a gentleman passenger's bag. He tells her to stop. The mother, very shocked at the man's behaviour, explains (at great length) the importance of freedom for little children.

As she continues defending her child, the metro arrives at a station, the doors open, and one of the children steps from the train. The doors close and the train pulls away. As it is about to enter the tunnel, the woman notices the child is missing and pulls the emergency lever.

The recently-rebuked passenger smiles and remarks, "But the child was only being free . . . !"

As mother and 5-year-old child walk past a display of kitchen units, the child heads for the units. Mother says, "Don't touch the cupboard doors. Don't touch the cupboard drawers." The child continues towards the display. Mother says, "Don't touch."

Child arrives at the display. Mother walks past the display on her way out of the shop saying, "Hey! Hallo!" Child opens and closes doors and drawers a number of times as mother does nothing to discipline her child for disobeying her, satisfied that the adorable child is free to touch and experience the cupboards.

In a supermarket, as mother is paying for food, child spots 10-cent plastic bags hanging by counter. Child helps itself to a bag. No reaction from mother. Child carries bag to mother and says, "Mama, I have a bag for you." Mother explains, "That's not allowed" (the popular DAT MAG NIET). Child ignores mother and mother ignores child. As mother packs her food away, child again offers her the bag. Mother explains further, "That's not allowed. THOSE COST PENNIES! That's why mama brought her own bag." Child ignores mother, clutching bag. Mother advises that she cannot keep the bag. Child begins to cry and eventually drops bag in a heap on the floor. Mother and screaming child walk away. Bag is left on the floor. No attempt is made by mother to pick/hang it up again.

Dat mag NIET . . .

Matériel

Throughout the period of infantile pampering, training aids are strategically introduced. The first, a ball, is presented before the art of walking has been mastered. The second, The Bicycle, is introduced shortly thereafter (by the age of 3, most mini-Netherlanders can ride a two-wheel Bike competently). Next comes mother's greatest gift (to herself and to the child): kindergarten. This can start anywhere between the age of 30 months and 5 years. Also during this period, children are awarded their first pair of ice skates, which are renewed annually.

The school years that follow shape their worldly views. Parents may select the school(s) their offspring attend. The choices available are based on classical education, philosophy and religion. Nowadays, classical education teaches the children to be "streetwise." Education based on philosophy is for *avant-garde* parents and has its roots buried in freedom of expression (with obvious results). Selection of a Christian school enables parents to segregate their children from Turks, Moroccans, etc., (who follow the Muslim faith) without being seen to be racist.

A catastrophe was narrowly averted when the Ministry of Education refused to grant random absence entitlement for school children (nipper-*snipperdagen*). Such holidays would supposedly have allowed parents more personal time with their offspring. Thankfully, the Ministry judged that the current entitlement of torture-*dagen* is more than any parent could realistically handle.

After-school hours (and school holidays) are a traditional period for children to "get even" for whatever minor injustices they feel have been inflicted upon them. Fueled by a thirst for revenge, the mini-mafia have in the past punished a whole generation by ringing doorbells and running away. This age-old prank has now been superseded by the act of *zapping* which is the clandestine art of roaming streets with a TV remote controller and resetting the TV volume, picture or channel setting when passing a viewer's house. When the electronics giant Philips was consulted for a possible cure, a spokesman declared:

> *There is no remedy. A television cannot distinguish between users with good intentions and users with bad intentions. We therefore recommend placing the television in a part of the abode that cannot be accessed that way.*

Great!

When full-time education is finally completed, the Dutch are suitably prepared for welfare or work (see Chapter 9). Parental pampering now diminishes, for the school-leavers are well versed in the art of babyhood.

Holland's Future

Ever since Holland became a welfare state in the 1960's, fewer and fewer Dutch children grow up wondering, *"What will my profession be when I grow up?"* Instead, they are brought up with the attitude, *"I will be taken care of."* And they are, by both Government and family, so that they (the children) can continue their magical mystery tour of life.

Twenty years on, the current herds of freeborn Dutch, with their divine qualities, will be the backbone of the country. They will be the mainstay of industry, the financiers and the politicians. Dutch kids, spawned by over-liberated mothers and welfare-minded fathers, will rule and govern the country. They will be steering the ship – a classic case of DUTCH HELM DISEASE.

A future Dutch Parliament?

chapter 7

CINEMA

C inema appeals to the Dutch. It is actively linked to the culture-vulture and individual-expression syndromes that all self-respecting Dutch persons acquire at birth. Unfortunately, their tenacity for over-respecting themselves, and under-respecting others, causes a total breakdown of consideration in the world of cinema. If you want to SEE and HEAR a feature film in Holland, wait for the video. If you merely wish to preview the decline and fall of civilization (as we know it), Dutch cinema *(bioscoop)* is for you.

Behaviour

1. The number one rule is that you must giggle, chatter, belch and rattle your candy wrappers as much as possible to ensure that no one can follow the film. If anyone's presence irritates you, throw your empty bottles and other rubbish at them while making loud and nasty comments about them.

2. If the theatre is not yet full, be sure to select a seat directly in front of someone else and to sit up as straight as possible (preferably with a tall hat on) to block their view. Better still, fidget frequently.

3. Make every effort to arrive late so as to inconvenience as many members of the audience as possible by blocking their view and stepping on their feet as you find a seat. If you have missed part of the film, ask the people sitting near you (in a loud voice) to explain in detail what has happened so far.

Intermission

The programme intermission provides a rest period for the audience:

1. Join the stampede to the foyer for obligatory coffee (to ease the throats of the better behaved), soft drinks or beer (to massage the throats of the worst behaved) and for restocking munitions of wrapped confectionery.

2. The middle ranks will remain in the theatre, rehearsing for the return game.

3. At the end of the intermission, smokers casually deposit still-smoldering cigarette ends in waste paper containers and all persons over 6 feet (1.9 metres) tall must delay returning to their seats until the programme has recommenced.

4. DO NOT even consider prematurely finishing a conversation to view the film.

Subtitles

When it comes to subtitles, the Dutch take the "sub" (meaning *of inferior quality*) to heart, excelling in their usual manner.

Imported cinema presentations are shown in their native language with Dutch subtitles. Many are of U.K. or U.S. origin. Native English speakers are misguided if they believe that comparison of the spoken word with the written word will further their knowledge of the Dutch tongue. The following translation rules are used:

- Make basic errors, such as translating 96 as 69, or 1959 as 1995.
- When it comes to translating humour, you must destroy any chance of the audience understanding what is going on.
- Don't bother to translate words (spelled the same, but with a different meaning) such as "gif(t)" (English = present; Dutch = poison) or "hare" (English = hare/rabbit; Dutch = her).

A Bad Case of the Clap

At the end of the show, the audience may actually burst into applause if the film is judged to be exceptionally entertaining.

After surviving cinema sadism, what better way to finish the evening than to adjourn to a local tavern to drink away your embarrassment of having clapped at a blank screen. Alas, other cinema patrons will have beaten you to the bar, and will be heavily engaged in interpreting, criticising and dissecting whatever parts of the film they might have managed to see and perhaps hear. The criticism is far-reaching, as Dutch film director Paul Verhoeven found to his cost:

> *[In Holland] there was tremendous resistance from the critics and the Producers Guild who made life unbearable. I was driven out of the country by the Producers Guild.*

A Concert Next Time?

If you are disenchanted with the cinema scenario, try a classical music concert for a contrasting experience. Various tactics are used to keep the audience quiet, such as the distribution of free cough drops. *"The throats of the visitors should be lubricated with the goal to silence the mouth,"* reads a notice at the Amsterdam **Concertgebouw**.

At the conclusion of the concert, a standing and thunderous ovation is given, irrespective of the quality of performance, in order to avoid *"understatement of the appreciation of concert performers,"* after which the concert is mercilessly analysed. The Dutch are extremely critical of musical conductors. At least one prominent conductor has resigned after repeated bowing to the plausible applause.

*They are frugal to the saving of eggshells and
maintain it for a maxime that a thing lasts
longer mended than new.*
Owen Feltham, London, 1652

*In matters of commerce the fault of the Dutch
is offering too little and asking too much.*
George Canning to Sir Charles Bagot,
British Minister, The Hague, 1826

chapter 8

MONEY

on gulden pond

T he unit of Dutch currency is called the guilder *(gulden)*,
logically abbreviated *HFl* or *f*. Higher denominations
(HFl 10- and up) are represented by inanely designed paper
notes, printed in equally inane colours. Lower denominations
consist of coins of various sizes, the smallest being the
10-cent piece *(dubbeltje)* which approximates the size of a
shirt button. The largest denomination coin is HFl 5-. It is not
the currency itself that has prompted the inclusion of this
chapter, but the manner in which it is revered.

DENOMINATION
CODE (FOR
BLIND PEOPLE)

DENOMINATION (AS IF THE COLOUR
SCHEME WAS NOT ENOUGH!)

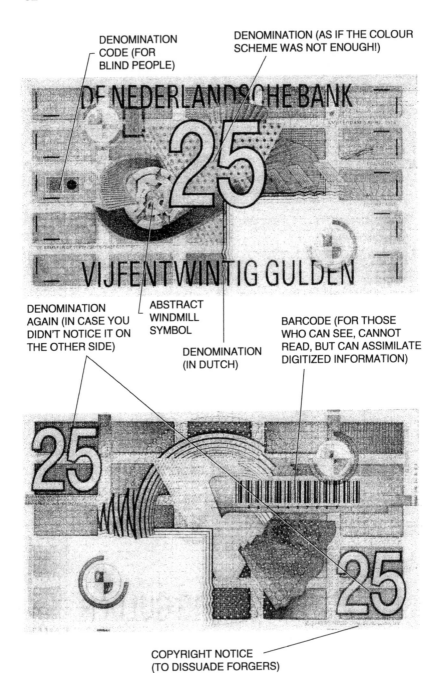

DENOMINATION
AGAIN (IN CASE YOU
DIDN'T NOTICE IT ON
THE OTHER SIDE)

ABSTRACT
WINDMILL
SYMBOL

BARCODE (FOR THOSE
WHO CAN SEE, CANNOT
READ, BUT CAN ASSIMILATE
DIGITIZED INFORMATION)

DENOMINATION
(IN DUTCH)

COPYRIGHT NOTICE
(TO DISSUADE FORGERS)

Cloggy cash

Bargain Hunting

The Dutch enjoy spending time going to various shops all over town in order to take advantage of special offers and sales. They will gladly spend an extra two hours shopping in order to save 5 cents on a can of beans. Some will even spend more on public transport than they save at the sale.

When shopping for clothes, they will search the racks and shelves, frantically looking for a slightly damaged or soiled article. This gives them licence to demand a price reduction. If they find one, they will purchase it whether it fits or not. It can always be used as a birthday present, or kept in storage for several years in case of weight gain or loss, or until their children grow into it.

In most of Europe, winter sales start in early January. In Holland, the sales begin towards the end of January. This eliminates the temptation for Dutch people to postpone Christmas until early January, thereby saving some of their precious pennies. January sales can be a violent experience in many countries. Risk the Dutch version at your peril.

All year round, sales and special offers abound, categorized as *uitverkoop* (sale); *aanbieding* and *aktie* (special offer); and *reclame* (advertised price, not to be confused with reclaimed land). None of these categories generate as much excitement as *alles moet weg* (everything must go).

A maze of complex and confusing rules governs price reductions *(reducties)*. Foreigners would require the equivalent of a master's degree on the subject to begin to understand how to manipulate the system. The Dutch appear to be born with this ability. As an example of the extent of the problem, no fewer than 19 different types of reduction were listed in the national railway guide for 1985-1986.

Street Markets

Every Dutch town or city has a deluge of street markets *(markt)*. Whether open daily or just once a week, regular attendance is compulsory for self-respecting *cloggies*, as this is where they find some of the best bargains. Members of all walks of life surface at the street market, and tourists should be advised that this is the place to go to:

- have your wallet stolen (if you haven't already managed to do so on the tram)
- see everyday Dutchmen wearing their famous wooden footwear *(klompen)*
- buy cheap imitation antiques, drugs, stolen goods and other miscellaneous merchandise
- experience the stench of rotting fish, vegetables and littered streets
- find yourself compacted among an endless throng of local tribespersons progressing at a snail's pace.

For local inhabitants, the street market is an exception to their rule of penurious shopping. They'll pay over the odds (within reason) for the privilege of shopping at their favourite stalls and market(s). The pilgrimage is not complete until they orate about the visit to their friends, neighbours, etc. This is also the one occasion where they refrain from bitching and whining about prices.

Second-hand Transactions

If you advertise the sale of second-hand items, you must expect to waste time over numerous long telephone calls probing for precise information on every imaginable detail about the *te koop* ("for sale") item(s). Even if the item has been sold, the callers will want to know all the details in order to find out if they have missed a good bargain.

Getting the price you quoted is a difficult feat, for in the words of Simon Schama reflecting on commerce in 17th-century Holland, *"In matters of bond, for example, they could be as slippery as the eels on which they supped."* To assist you in dealing with the Dutch barter martyrs, the following guidelines are offered:

1. COMPROMISE them before they compromise you. Upon entering your home, the prospective buyer will take an instant mental inventory in order to select a conversation piece to steer the topic in his favour. The ensuing discussion is used to prepare you for the I-can't-afford-that-price speech.

2. ATTITUDE. Adopt the firm attitude that the advertised price is the only acceptable price. Ignore arguments that the item can be purchased at a lower price at the local market. If that were the case, the prospective buyer would not have wasted his precious money and time on the phone call and journey.

3. CHANGE SYNDROME. Every good *cloggy* will arrive with money strategically distributed about his person. If the quoted price was HFl 40-, a successful transaction will unfold as follows:

- One pocket or compartment will contain HFl 30-, one will contain HFl 10- and one will contain a single note of HFl 100- or more.
- Upon eventual agreement of the price (HFl 40-), the buyer will produce HFl 30- and rummage around to discover the HFl 100- note, assuming that you will not have change for the large note.
- This would appear to be the crucial moment. Do you risk losing the sale if you maintain your price, or call his bluff?
- You call his bluff. After a further reluctant rummage, he will produce the crumpled HFl 10- note. You are happy to receive the full price. The buyer is content knowing that he gave you a good run for his money.

Shelling Out for Fuel

When the Dutch buy gasoline, they don't fill their tanks; they buy in multiples of 5 litres. For each 5 litres you purchase, you get one savings stamp *(spaarzegel)*. To fill the tank regularly may result in the loss of two or three stamps over a few months! A full card of *spaarzegels* (approx. 40) can be cashed-in for the monetary equivalent of 3.33 litres of gasoline. Alternatively, you can elect to receive a special (read: trashy) gift.

Fines

Fines are fine for fine people. In Holland, an intricate system exists whereby the State levies fines encompassing such common misdemeanours as illegal entry and parking offences.

When you see arriving passengers being interrogated by the police at Schiphol airport customs, you will probably assume they are drug dealers. Wrong. Chances are they forgot to pay a parking ticket during their last stay in Holland.

Pay your parking tickets if you ever plan to return to Holland! If you fail to pay a ticket and attempt to enter the country at a later date, you run a high risk of being detained by the police at the port of entry. They will require you to pay for the ticket, even if it's years old, plus a fine.

Pay your fines!

The same applies if you inadvertently miss paying your last rubbish collection bill or if your residency permit expires while you are outside the country. When you re-enter, you will likely be invited to the 'explanation chamber.'

This restitution justifies the Government's outlay on "high tech" equipment such as computers, multi-channel synthesized hand-held transceivers, etc.

Banks

In general, the banks are efficiently and professionally run. They would be. The Dutch would have it no other way.

Personal experience indicates that debit transactions are balanced on a daily basis while credits are acknowledged up to seven days after the fact.

Given the public's appreciation of orderly queuing, bank branches tend to issue numbered tickets when the complement of clients totals one or more. As a bonus, this system eliminates the possibility of labeling the bank undemocratic, sexist, racist or withdrawal-ist. Bank staff can adopt as unhelpful an attitude as possible:

Can I have a transfer form?
No.
Why?
We don't give out blank ones anymore.

(At this point play them at their own game:)

Can you type my account information onto a blank one, and give me the form to take away?
Yes, naturally!

Cashiers are most helpful in one respect: They happily share confidential banking information, such as your bank balance, with all within earshot. Once again, Dutch openness prevails.

A Sporting Chance?

The Dutch love to be associated with sporting activities, provided the cost is not too high.

On a skiing vacation, they will insist (from the very first lesson) on zigzagging their way down the slopes. After all, they have paid for the journey to the top and must therefore extract maximum value from the journey down.

The laws of magnetism dictate that the Dutch will be attracted to mountain climbing. Having no such natural features, they improvise by climbing man-made vertical barriers, such as an underpass ret(r)aining wall near the Amstel Station, Amsterdam. This activity, of course, is free of charge as the walls were erected for other purposes. It provides an authentic training ground; after all, everyone knows that 20th-century architecture strongly resembles the snow-encrusted peaks of the Alps and the Himalayas.

When they fish, they religiously use two rods: Their fishing permit allows a maximum of two rods. Any fewer would be abusing their purse by not getting their money's worth.

Football *(voetbal)* is the national sport. TV programmes are canceled without warning to show matches. If their team wins the cup, the whole town gets drunk. If they lose, the whole town gets drunk.

Ice skating is another extremely popular sport, in large part due to the fact that anyone can skate for free on the numerous canals, ditches and other waterways.

Hot rodding

The Baud Bunch

Personal computers have evolved as an entertainment-cult throughout the western world. The Dutch characteristically resisted the electronic invasion for years (see Chapter 3). When anarchic Bulletin Boards evolved to link dedicated users throughout Europe and North America in the 1980s, Rip van Winkle awoke. One of the most popular Bulletin Board systems of the era was "FidoNet," and its November 1987 listing of "nodes" quoted:

W. Germany	Italy	Holland	U.K.
Pop. 60 million	Pop. 54.5 million	Pop. 14.6 million	Pop. 55 million
26 nodes	26 nodes	104 nodes	67 nodes

Perhaps the reason for the tremendous success of the baud brigade in Holland is that this breed of Bulletin Board invariably provided for the acquisition of crude and largely useless information, programs, games, etc., FREE OF CHARGE.

Once hooked by an attack of the freebie-jeebies, there was no stopping 'em. Cohorts of *cloggy* keystroke cops infested cyberspace as FidoNet begat the CompuServe clan of "on-line services" and later THE INTERNET and its WORLD WIDE WEB. During this transition, the world was blessed with a Dutch edition of the PC Magazine On-line Forum – perhaps not a modem megahit, but certainly a forum for 'em. Forced back into the paying pattern, the newly computer-literate lap-top layabouts celebrated this global breakthrough with stimulating postings such as: *"Een shit bulletin board"* and intellectual responses such as [translated], *"Typical of an anonymous, socially-handicapped adolescent who probably uses fraudulent credit card data to join the forum. The only people to profit from this are the PTT."*

The Dutch have since spawned some of the most adept "hackers," forever foraging for networks and services to infiltrate. A successful intrusion affords them their fifteen minutes of fame and allows them to once again . . .

_____

*. . . get something they don't want
for free!*

_____

In Times of Sadness

The most unsavoury aspect of the "Guilder Builder" characteristic manifests itself when tragedy strikes.

A Dutch funeral is an occasion where the Dutch excel at money-related cold-mindedness. A recently bereaved spouse or parent must be ever-cautious to the profiteering of funeral organizers. In the event that you are unfortunately placed in this position, recruit the aid of a *cloggy*. He/she will guard you against:

- overpriced floral tributes (expect a 200-300% price increase on usually-cheap bouquets of flowers, when ordered for funeral purposes)
- overpriced coffee (while your only thought is to lay your loved one to rest with dignity, care and respect, your aide will embark on a debate over the funeral arranger's price-per-head for coffee and cookies, compared with the local café)
- the futility of paying extra for piped music if you think nobody will be listening to it.

Afterwards the whole congregation adjourns to the abode of the next-of-kin for a drunken and relentless round of bickering and bartering over the spoils.

1991 saw a revolutionary law introduced regarding body disposal: Cremations and burials would be allowed without the necessity of a coffin. Among the most critical were (of course) the funeral establishments who were horrified at the prospect of their main source of mark-up disappearing:

"It is wonderful that the lawmakers want to please the minorities, but there has been no consideration for the crematorium employees and what it means to cremate

*an uncoffined body – a body bursts into flames, and that
is not a pretty sight!"*
A graveyard president complained, *"You can't just
throw a sheet over a body . . . ,"* then suggested, *". . .
maybe we can lay it on a plank!"*

Why?

When confronted with the charge of fanatical frugality,
the average *cloggy* cites CALVINISM! as the root cause, then
continues to practice the guilder gospel. No attempt is
made to shed the yolk of the archaic moralistic code. This
is perhaps the only example of the Dutch accepting a
principle such as predestination without question or protest. And why not -- it's good for the purse.

The Dutch version of Calvinism is to:

- Guard every cent you own, and fight for every
  cent you can make.
- Deny, hide or apologize for your wealth to anyone that enquires of it.
- Plead poverty at all times.

This is a far cry from the original doctrine: *". . . to learn
to submit themselves to God, they must first be stripped of their
wealth."*

Try these examples if you are ever unfortunate enough
to be in a position worthy of their use:

1. If you must buy expensive clothes, don't discuss
   the quality. Instead, mention the good bargain
   you got, thus making the garments seem less
   expensive than they were.

2. To someone who remarks on the obvious luxury of your home, reply, *"Yes, it is a big house, but in fact a bit too large and luxurious for us. Had we realized how costly it would be, we would certainly have bought something more modest."*

3. When hosting a lavish party, ask your guests to make a contribution for the coffee, as if you can't really afford the gala affair.

4. On a luxury cruise, openly display your membership to The Loud and Proud Crowd by placing yourself above rules of etiquette and common decency.

5. On returning from the luxury cruise, criticize insignificant details, giving the impression that you've been on a cheap package tour.

*We believe you must give people a basic
wage, and let them choose whether
or not to work.*
Gerrit Jan Wolffensperger,
senior Amsterdam council member

chapter 9

UITKERING

the dutch work ethic

If you truly want to integrate with Dutch society, you must
have at least one type of *uitkering* (welfare, national
assistance; pronounced "out-caring").

Applying for welfare and reaping the benefits is not a
social disgrace – it is a right. (In 1986, one quarter of the
population of Amsterdam was on welfare.) Those governmental bureaucrats whose role in life is to approve your
uitkering will give you all the assistance you require, to the
point of helping you re-write your application to receive
maximum payment. If you don't qualify by answering *JA*

(yes), then answer *NEEN* (no), the social worker will likely advise.

The System I - Methodology

Basically, there is only one requirement to obtain your *uitkering*: you must be prepared to spend a long time in the dismal, unventilated waiting room(s) on numerous frustrating occasions.

Advantages of having an *uitkering* are as follows:

- It kills any incentive you may have had to work. This is excellent training for the Dutch youth.
- It gives the Dutch Government an excuse to have one of the highest tax rates in the world.
- It attracts thousands of foreigners, especially Turks and Moroccans (so the Dutch can prove they aren't racist).
- It encourages those who get the urge to work to do so illegally to supplement their income. This is known as "black" *(zwart)* work by those who engage in it and "white" *(wit)* fraud by welfare institutions. Be careful which term you use when speaking with strangers.
- It encourages many to live abroad on welfare benefits at the expense of those who pay taxes.

Although Holland has one of the most comprehensive welfare systems and superior national health programmes, and even though there is almost no true poverty in the country, the natives still voice their disapproval. They want more. And they want it free *(gratis)*. Many women, youths and foreigners have rallied behind the motto *Bijstand Mis$tand* (Welfare = $-Abuse). Others have interpreted *Bijstand Mis$tand* to indicate their opposition to welfare because it makes people dependent and therefore is a "capitalist slave-making system." The point here is that the Dutch themselves cannot agree on the meaning of the motto around which they rally.

Some cities publish a free monthly newspaper for welfare recipients. The publications provide them with all the latest benefits they are entitled to receive, demonstration dates/locations and ways to manipulate the system.

Abuses withstanding, the system DOES provide help for the genuinely underprivileged, the chronically ill, the elderly and children in a far better and more humanitarian manner than the various so-called *"social security programmes"* which operate in many other western countries.

Work Attitude

Despite the attraction of a generous unemployment benefit, some choose to actually work for a living. The idea here is to impress your employer for a period of three months after which it is practically impossible for him to dismiss you, as will be seen later.

During the probationary period, you will without doubt experience some frustration regarding the lack of effort extended by your colleagues. However, once you complete your three months, your working life takes on a completely different character. You belong.

You can now concentrate more on the "social aspects of work." Work now interrupts coffee breaks. A heated, two-hour debate over the validity of your boss's order receives higher priority than the five-minute task of executing it. A colleague's birthday takes top priority. The important event allows various workers to arrange a collection, purchase celebration requisites and organize the compulsory office "SURPRISE" party. You, as birthday boy/girl *(jarige)*, are not left out as it is your duty to provide edible delights. The party, of course, takes place during company hours. It is left to the reader's discretion to fantasize the effects of (say) the Olympic Games in Holland.

Good timekeeping is no longer a matter of conscience. Remember that the Dutch form of the expression *"The early bird catches the worm"* is:

"The early bird is for the cat."

Dismissal --
Failure or Success?

An employer must give you a "reasonable" (but unspecified) amount of verbal warnings as to your misconduct. Next, three written warnings must be issued (on separate occasions). These are only officially recognized if you (the accused) acknowledge acceptance in writing. Without your acceptance, the matter goes to arbitration.

With your signature, the case is presented to the local authorities for assessment and possible authorized dismissal. The word "possible" is used here meaningfully. Should the authorities decide your dismissal is valid, your new-found unemployed status will inevitably qualify you for welfare. Welfare through unemployment is typically 70% of your last salary, paid by the same local authority (1992). Given the Dutch affinity to the guilder (see Chapter 8), it follows that the local authority will be hesitant to approve a dismissal.

At work, employees have little or no fear of being fired. They can basically do what they want. If they don't like a particular task, they refuse to do it. Some days or weeks later when their supervisor asks them how the project is progressing, the employee(s) typically reply with a shrug and inhale the word *"Ja!?!"*

If for one reason or another you find you are experiencing stress on the job, one of the most popular and successful tactics is to stage a nervous breakdown and go on paid sick leave for several months. By the time you return, your employer will either have you work harder than ever to catch up, thereby putting you under stress again, or will ask you to resign. The answer will likely be a negotiated settlement wherein your disappearance is rewarded by a large payment made in such a manner that your welfare claims are not compromised.

You can have quite a nice time working in Holland!

Subsidies

Generous subsidies of all types are available. The most common is the housing subsidy *(huursubsidie)*. Also widespread are educational grants and subsidies. These include the arts. Often the financial encouragements are in the form of a purchase of the subject matter by the Government, in order to help the aspiring artists. Some of the works are displayed in a multitude of public buildings for all common taxpayers to savour. The rest (the greater majority) are stuffed away in storage while their owners offer daily prayers that the works will achieve masterpiece status in later decades. In 1973, a psychiatrist was subsidized to

A work of art?

pose on a pedestal in a museum, proclaiming himself to be a work of art. (Hopefully he also was hung in a multitude of buildings.)

Life is based in large part around the amount and types of subsidies one receives. Recipients carefully weigh the financial consequences of starting part-time or full-time work. A job seriously affects their welfare and subsidies.

Time-off

Every person recognized by the social security system, employed or otherwise, bank president or street sweeper, is entitled to a minimum of 25 days holiday *(vakantie)* each year. This may seem overly generous until you consider that a large part of the holiday pay *(vakantiegeld)* is deducted from the individual's wages throughout the year and paid back during the holiday period together with the employer's contribution, after taxation. Thus the thrifty Dutch award about four weeks' holiday and pay for roughly half – a classic example of *"going Dutch."* Again, it is the *uitkering*-ites who win, as they receive a bonus with their welfare payments for four weeks of the year.

Sick leave is yet another way to maximize an employee's welfare benefits. When you report an illness, representatives are sent to your home about once a week to "confirm" that you are at home and are genuinely ill. The visits are only allowed to take place during specified hours (Monday to Friday, mornings until 10 and afternoons from 12 to 2:30) of the first three weeks of your illness.

This procedure rightly allows the critically ill sufficient latitude to shop for the necessities of life, such as flowers and coffee, without the fear of losing any welfare entitlement.

The System II -- Consequences

Based on 1992 statistics, some consequences of the foregoing "reasoning" are as follows:

- By the year 2005, more people will receive an *uitkering* than those who work (Ministry of Social Affairs).
- Between 50,000 and 90,000 of the legal residents have no health insurance.
- There were more than 900,000 people listed as *"disabled"* in 1991 (*"disabled"* benefits are some of the most lucrative types).
- The Netherlands has the most part-time jobs in the western world.

chapter 10

MET WIE?

identification & telephone habits

Official Documents

If you spend more than a few days in Holland, you will undoubtedly be baffled by the Dutch obsession with paraffin (misspelled, *parafen*). Indeed, the word appears on most Dutch documents.

A Dutch *paraaf* (signing of initials) consists of one or more large, illegible scribbles, used mainly to ensure that no one but the originator can decipher the initials. The formal signature (*handtekening*, lit. "hand-drawing") is equally as enigmatic as the initials, only there is more of it. Whether using the *paraaf* or hand-drawing, the process of bold and daring scribbling provides positive identification of the Dutch nationality.

Of equal importance on some documents is the *stempel* (rubber stamp). While some documents require only a *paraaf*, others need the hand-drawing and yet others need the "stamp." Sometimes a combination of *stempel* + *paraaf* or stamp + hand-drawing are necessary.

Place and Date

Other vital ingredients of a legal Dutch document include the date and place *(datum en plaats)*, despite the fact that the place can easily be falsified and is inconsequential.

I.D.-ology
(proof of identification)

When the Dutch bark *"legitimatie"* at you, for once they are not being rude; they are not probing into your family history or parentage. The word is harmless, meaning "identification."

The Dutch alien residence card *(verblijfskaart)*, issued to non-Dutch dwellers LEGALLY residing in the Netherlands, requires strong proof of identity and purpose for its issuance. Yet this card is not considered a form of identification by most institutions, including the post office, even though it bears your name, photo, hand-drawing, birth date, place of birth, nationality and alien registration number, verified by a minimum of two *stempels* and an official hand-drawing by an authorized member of the alien police. Additional space is provided on the card for

Dutch paraffin | Hand-drawings

"notes," each of which is duly stamped, dated and initialed by an officer.

Introductions

When being introduced to a Dutch person for the first time, a mutual monotone mumbling of names takes place. Expressions such as, *"How do you do?" "Pleased to meet you,"* etc., are not used. During the introduction, your gaze should be a vacant one. Avoid eye contact.

Hand contact, called "hand-giving" *(hand geven)*, consists of a nervous, damp, limp, hand wobble (see Chapter 14). The facial expression is one of boredom and indifference.

Telephone Manners

In Holland, you must state your name every time you answer your phone. If you fail to do so, the other party will either lapse into silence or demand to know who you are *(Met wie spreek ik?)* before uttering another word. *Cloggies* are seemingly incapable of holding any type of telephone conversation without knowing your name:

> *Can I speak to Mr. van Doorn?*
> **What is your name?**
> *John Smith.*
> (Bluntly) ***Ja! The switchboard is closed. Call back later.***
> *Can I leave my name or a message?*
> **No!**

Many Dutch suffer from telephonophobia *(telefoonvrees)*. The symptoms include anxiety and extreme nervousness when dealing with both incoming and outgoing calls. The Dutch are at a loss to explain the origin of their phone fear, but admit it is not unknown for the weak-hearted to go into cardiac arrest at the sound of a ringing phone. An answerphone only makes things worse, including the word for the associated affliction: *telefoonbeantwoorderapparaatvrees*.

Perhaps one cause of their telephonophobia is that deep in the subconscious mind, they all know what to expect when dealing with calls to or from a business, public office, etc. . . . If you try to obtain a piece of information, you get passed from one number to another. After four or five frustrating calls, each time repeating your name and request, you are fortunate if you reach the correct office.

To add to the inbred paranoia, the national telephone service (PTT) intends to implement a more efficient system of informing subscribers about the possibility of "eavesdropping." Telephone directories, price lists, etc., would advise the general public that their calls can be "bugged." Car phone services, which are particularly prone to frequent, undetectable "bugging," may be modified to include a prerecorded warning at the start of every incoming call. George Orwell would love it.

If you do not know the toadstool (*toestel* or extension number) or department (*afdeling*), it will be necessary to explain in great detail to the switchboard operator why you are calling, and why you are calling THEM. Just as you reach the interesting part of your lengthy explanation, the operator, not knowing what on earth you are talking about, will either:

- cut you off, or
- connect you to a toadstool, seemingly selected at random. When someone answers, you must begin your explanation all over again . . . and again . . . and again . . . .

When you ring the police, expect to have a long wait until someone replies. Offer the burglar or murderer in your home a cup of coffee to stall him while you wait for the police to answer your call.

In order to lessen the trauma of the general population over their phobia, plush public telephone booths are placed at convenient locations throughout the country. These structures are not so much provided for the purpose of making telephone calls, but for the therapeutic exercise of "hypervandalism." By daylight, the telephone directory (if it has not been stolen or otherwise removed) can be destroyed and replaced with graffiti -- written and sprayed from floor to roof, inside and out. When darkness descends and the general public has had time to read the graffiti, all windows and other breakable components (including the apparatus itself) can be destroyed. On weekends, the booth can be set on fire.

The (Dutch) urge to be original often leads to utter nonsense . . .
Han Lammers,
Queen's Commissioner for
Flevoland Province

chapter 11

THE NATIONAL PASSION

The Dutch love to devote time to a "good cause." They express their devotion in the form of demonstrations, riots, debate, discussions and the inevitable collections. The common denominator is PROTEST.

When these gentle pacifists are inconvenienced or their egos ruffled, they instinctively resort to aggression and/or violence of tongue and word. (They rarely resort to acts of physical violence as such behaviour is abhorred by the population as a whole.) They get their way -- more so than any other nation. But it's never enough for them. They always find more to COMPLAIN and PROTEST about. This perpetual cycle of confrontation and inherent change has been instrumental in reducing excesses of the wealthy and powerful. Consequently, class distinction is minimal. The philosophy would appear to be:

- We hate anybody telling us what to do.
- Speak out! (At times the Government and law enforcement agencies are paralysed by the thought: "People would not stand for it.")
- Defy defiance.

Defiance is found even in the isolated areas where rigid rules and strict moral discipline reign. In 1971 in the ultra-conservative village of Staphorst, where polio vaccination was always strongly advised against by the local church authorities, most parents had their children inoculated during a polio epidemic.

A favourite method of self-expression is the use of "profound" slogans and/or maxims. These are often presented in the form of pathetically unsubtle jingles, such as *"GEEN WONING, GEEN KRONING"* (no housing, no coronation) on the occasion of the crowning of Queen Beatrix in 1980, or *"WONEN NIET SPELEN"* (housing, not games), when the city of Amsterdam was a candidate for the 1992 Olympic Games. Such sayings are displayed in various ways:

- GRAFFITI. Graffiti is used as a means of bringing the message to the masses. It can be found in abundance at places where the public gather. Main transport termini, (surviving) telephone booths and church walls are popular bulletin boards.
- BUTTONS. Featuring the established slogan or maxim for the cause, handwritten and often including a crude cartoon-like illustration or motif,

these are conspicuously displayed on the clothing of sympathizers and supporters of the cause as medals of service. It is not uncommon for the chest of the enlightened bearer to be adorned with a multitude of different campaign buttons, thereby giving indication of rank to the protesting legions.

- STICKERS. Stickers are designed much as the buttons, but somewhat less abundant, probably due to the relatively high cost of production.
- BANNERS. These are usually made from old bed sheets and house paint and are erected or hung from the roof top or windows of a protester's home or headquarters on the day of the official protest. Thereafter the device is left in place to rot, as a symbol of freedom and remembrance to all disinterested parties.

A slogan-sticker: "I do it with (a condom)"

- PROMOTIONAL T-SHIRTS. These tend to embody
  more patronizing phraseology such as those
  used to promote the 1992 Amsterdam Olympics
  with the slogan: *"Holland wants the world to win."*
  (Holland and the world lost – the 1992 Olympics
  were held elsewhere.)

The tide began to change in the late 1980's when some
groups decided that slogans don't work anymore. Instead,
these groups elected to write and analyse thorough annual
reports in order to impress politicians and the police.

The Dutch attention span is in some respects short-
lived. In such a radically progressive and rapidly changing
nation, it is no wonder that every few years each new wave
of youth rejects the ideas of the previous. In this sense,
labeling a cause or movement as old-fashioned discredits it
and serves as an insult to any lingering, faithful followers.

Discussion and Debate

In the earliest and calmest phases, the national passion
is disseminated through discussion and debate. Whenever
and wherever more than one *cloggy* is present, they will
engage in what they consider to be deep and meaningful
discussion. They cannot stop themselves. In the office,
meetings drag on endlessly since so much attention is
given to the right to fully express one's personal opinion.
The impression that something was actually settled in a
meeting will be proven wrong when workers later remark,

We didn't agree to anything yet. We only discussed it.

This famously frustrating phrase prompts many to exclaim, *"Let's stop TALKING about it and DO something!"* and
is summed up by the classic maxim:

It is better to debate a question without settling it than to settle a question without debating it.

Cloggies like to interject a good dose of body language into their discussions, as illustrated by the following *"Jan & Piet"* joke:

Jan had been expounding his views to his colleague Piet on a winter day. After a while, Jan said, *"You do the talking for a while, Piet. My hands are cold."*

Complain, Protest, Object, Appeal

When discussion and debate do not settle a problem, Hollanders escalate to the next phase where they voice their disapproval through the accepted and sacred channels of COMPLAINT, PROTEST, OBJECTION and APPEAL.

When the Dutch disagree with something, the first step is to COMPLAIN. COMPLAIN to anyone who will listen. Grumbling and COMPLAINING are part of the Dutch way of life.

Having found sympathetic ears, the next step in the process is to PROTEST. With the support of the ears and their associated mouths, the PROTEST can be made known to the offending party. This is usually accomplished through the medium of the written word.

Only when the PROTEST is met with overwhelming apathy does the disagreement gain momentum. The sym-

pathetic ears and mouths now become an offended action
(aktie) group, and the disagreement automatically enters
the OBJECTION phase. This phase is an overzealous form of
the PROTEST and can include pleas, threats, demands and
anything else that would likely win the day. The more
determined objectors arrange for details of their dispute to
be included in specialist community publications.

The final conflict is manifested as the APPEAL. To win it
requires all the support and cunning a Dutch(wo)man can
muster. The APPEAL is a battle of wits and manœuvring in
both written and verbal form. (When a Dutch neighbour
was once asked for advice about a dispute, she advised,
"Je moet nu een grote mond opzetten," – lit., *"Now you have
to open your mouth wide."*)

This four-element procedure is followed at all levels –
official and unofficial, domestic and bureaucratic. It is valid

Appealing – Dutch style

in the case of an inconsiderate neighbour. Similarly, most official letters dealing with governmental finances end with a clause stating that YOU HAVE THE RIGHT TO OBJECT (*bezwaar indienen*) to the Government's decision. Even the annual income tax form states, *"After some time you will receive a reply to your letter of objection. If you do not agree with this reply, you can appeal."* You usually have 1-2 months to APPEAL. Depending on the circumstances, your letter can be sent to the office in question, or to the mayor or the Queen.

Causes

The causes, protests and incessant gum-bashing about "opinion" are all done in the name of freedom and the Dutch concept of democracy. As soon as the suffix *-vrij* (free) is added to a noun depicting a supposed evil force, the word is sanctified and warrants flagrant public display, for example, *"kernwapenvrije gemeente"* (nuclear weapon-free community) and *"rookvrij gebouw"* (non-smoking building).

Although the Dutch will scrimp and save every last cent, morsel of food or scrap of clothing whenever possible, they do like to give, but only to what they consider to be a worthwhile cause. This is usually through an organized foundation *(stichting)* with tax-free status.

A *FUND FOR RELIEF FROM PERSECUTION AND EUTHANASIA OF AMPHI-EROTIC, ONE-LEGGED MICE IN THE SOUTHERN PROVINCE OF WESTERN ZILDENAVIA* would give the Dutch pride in their worldly consideration. Such a cause would be supported as totally justified as it encompasses the following (Dutch readers, please note that the order presented is alphabetical and in no way politically or emotionally prejudiced):

- gay rights
- handicapped rights
- lesbian rights
- rodent rights
- trend factor (popular since the 1970's: "We hate America(ns)," anti-nuclear all, euthanasia, etc.)
- unfamiliar location/ethnic rights.

This cause will warrant demonstrations, riots and, most important of all, collections. Donations will inevitably be void of taxation.

The logic behind the attitude is described in promotional material from an Utrecht *aktie* group:

Actions, in which and through which, people are offered the opportunity to take action themselves.

Any legal resident of Holland may hold a demonstration. It is a democratic right. Whether it is supported by five or 50,000, it is allowed to take place. Demonstrations must be well organized and co-ordinated with the local authorities. Every town or city has its own rules for this activity. Specifically, you must inform the local police of the intended date, time and especially the GOAL of the event, after which you will be advised of any necessary modifications to:

- date and time, which will be changed if any previously-approved demonstrations or civic events conflict with your plans
- route, which will be changed or streets closed to traffic, depending on the anticipated support for the cause.

When all is agreed, you will receive your demonstration permit and the necessary preparations can be made for the day. During the demonstration, you will naturally notice increased police presence. Do not be dismayed. They are individuals first and policemen second. Some will even gladly display your campaign button on their uniform. If so requested, police car(s) will follow your demonstration along its defined route to ensure your cause is heard and not disrupted.

Non-approved demonstrations are not permitted, but are often allowed if they are orderly and do not disturb traffic – and depending on the appearance of the protesters and the general acceptance of the goal. Police support during the proceedings is limited.

It must be emphasized that many of the causes have the good of the nation, minorities, the oppressed or all of (wo)mankind in mind. Whatever the subject matter, they are an ongoing example of democracy in progress. What appears to be a Dutch addiction to this process strikes visitors to the country as rather curious. Perhaps these passionate demonstrations and debates account in part for the relatively low level of violence in an increasingly violent era.

Demonstrating and protesting first became popular and fashionable following World War II. Many 60+ers do not appreciate such activities. As one overseas correspondent writes,

> *This type of thing is not dignified and not in line with the traditional sobriety of the Dutch. It is more a recent phenomenon which may well disappear as time goes by. I personally hope so, as I would hate this trend to become a Dutch characteristic.*

'The Dutch Way'

The most successful of Dutch causes are elevated to the rank of "The Dutch Way," which is an adulation bestowed upon those principles and prejudices that command the support of 250% of the population. In this respect, the housing rights issue of the 1970's and 1980's commands the prime example. Long-suffering parents were anxious for their post-pubic offspring to vacate the nest while the *enfants terribles* themselves could not wait to feather their own nests. But there are few empty homes.

A typically Dutch answer to this situation was to form pressure groups known to the outside world as *krakers*. The *krakers*, who enjoyed their heyday in the 1980's, fanatically opposed the acquisition of empty buildings for speculation – all reasonable and uninhabited space should be translated into subsidized housing for them. This is "The Dutch Way."

Krakers invaded vacant places: office blocks, individual flats, shops, warehouses or any other construction that was vacant for more than a few days. The *kraker*-cause came to a head during violent riots in Amsterdam. The police were forced to call in the army which brought in a tank to move the crowd. The confrontation ended only when the city agreed to renovate the occupied building for the squatters. *"We have the squatters under control now . . ."* A city housing official summed it up by stating that the job would cost more than a million guilders, *". . . an expensive way to deal with a little social unrest. But it's The Dutch Way."*

The *krakers* have since dropped from the limelight, their particular cause appearing old-fashioned to the masses. A 1991 attempt to revive public support by invading a small island was met with little more than a sarcastic smirk by the general populace and a request from the *Rijkswaterstaat* to "kindly vacate the premises."

No doubt partially due to the support and success of the *krakers'* tactics in Amsterdam, RaRa *(de Revolutionaire Anti Racistische Actie)* exploded terrorist bombs at the Amsterdam home of the Secretary of State and at the Palace of Justice in The Hague in 1991. The cause in question was a series of governmental proposals on reforming political asylum and its abuse. Public reaction was one of outrage and horror, giving hope to all that this kind of senseless anti-Dutch activity will NOT become The NEW Dutch Way.

The House of Her

Women's liberation is probably the most extreme example of the "National Passion" that readily demonstrates (sorry, exemplifies) itself. And no wonder. The Dutch Government willingly provides 12-13 million guilders annually for feminists to do "research." The modern Dutch *Vrouwen* (women) are so fanatical about their genetic characteristics that they elevate femininity to the highest pinnacle possible. They are WOMEN -- and people, humans, etc., secondly. *Vrouwen* have their own *cafés*, books, magazines, newspapers, theatres, travel agencies, unions and, of course, their own therapy centres. Through these media, *Vrouwen* can, and do, form many pressure groups which effect radical changes to society and its laws, on such subjects as birth control, abortion, divorce, homosexuality and equality-through-dominance.

Vrouwen-causes are a classic and typical obsession with which the modern Dutch identify. Any variety can trigger a chain reaction with the hope of achieving the ultimate goal of a Europe-wide demonstration against things that ordinary people would class as petty fads. As an indication of the severity of the infliction, the 1987 Amsterdam Telephone Directory listed no less than 27 entries under *"Vrouwen"* alone. Amongst the more paranoid were:

- *Vrouwen Actiecomité van Vervroegd AOW-Pens.* (Women's action committee for early old-age pensions)
- *De Vrouwenfietsenmakerij* (Women's Bicycle Repairer)
- *Stichting Aktiekomitée Vrouwen in de Bijstand* (Women's welfare action committee foundation)
- *Vrouwenklussenkollektief de Karweiven* (Women's Odd-Jobs Collective – the "Female Odd-Jobs")
- *Internationaal Archief v.d. Vrouwenbeweging* (International archives of women's movements), which boasts of 45,000 volumes (mostly in Dutch) of gender-related information.

While gathering background material for this chapter, we attempted to contact 33 women's organizations in order to ascertain their goals. Of the enquiries dispatched:

- Twenty were never answered.
- Three were returned, unopened.
- Nine replied, enclosing details of their craft and promotional brochures, obligatory stickers, etc.
- One replied by postcard, demanding to know, *". . . who you are, how you got our address, where you learned dutch and what you are going to do with the information . . . ."*

So much for the feminists' desire to make their suffering known to the whole of man- and woman-kind. Typical of the mentality reflected in the replies we did receive:

". . . we are not against anything. We demand the right to live according to the custom of this country and not to be seen as half of a couple but as an individual person and be treated as such."

MORE NOW FOR VROUW

The custom of the country being that man goes to work, WOMAN remains home with children and housework.

Despite suffragette-like campaigns, the greater cause of Dutch **Vrouwen**-freedom can only succeed if blessed with governmental cash. STEO (Stimulation Group for Liberation Research) asks HFl 6 million annually for *"Vrouwen-studies,"* and **Management Emacipatie** (formed to improve the position of women in career instructions) asks for a budget of HFl 7.3 million.

Ironically, in their struggle for equality and dominance, many Dutch women emulate and incorporate the very masculine characteristics which they claim they despise. These characteristics have been *vrouwen*ed upon by concerned males for over three centuries:

. . . In their families they are all equals and you have no way to know the master and mistress but by taking them in bed together!

Owen Feltham, London, 1652

. . . Most of the women there (Holland) have no taste, are most unfeminine, and walk like farmers!

Hans Algra, South Africa, 1992

Domestic bliss à la vrouw.

Finally on this topic, an extract from a pamphlet supplement issued by the Amsterdam Migrant's Center is included here in its ORIGINAL, unabridged English language form:

> . . . And a last example, in which the center did not play a role: Amsterdam house wives became a lot more critical on the quality of the vegetables on market places having noticed how the Surinam, Turkish and Moroccan migrants make their choise. The daily supply of previously unknown vegetables proves the influence of the new cuisines on Dutch cooking.

(Answers on a postcard, please, to . . .)

Military Service

Until 1995, Dutch military service was compulsory and limited to just over a one-year period for young males. Now it is strictly a volunteer affair. To some its hardship equals that of a stay in a holiday camp. The ranks are permitted to retain long hair, earrings and other symbols of their mid-childhood, and enjoy full labour benefits (controlled working hours, public holidays, etc.). Even the officers have a union contract. Gays are welcome and received at all entry levels, as an inquiry in the early 1970's found homosexual exclusion to be discriminatory.

Back in the not-so-distant days of conscription, the alternative to military service was to become a conscientious objector, officially recognized and categorized. A *dienst weigeraar* (service "refuser") performed civilian-type work, or a *totaal weigeraar* (complete "refuser") lounged around in a military prison for about two years. Even after sentencing, a *weigeraar* could conscientiously object – and still have a chance of beating the system. One such *totaal weigeraar* was freed from captivity after 24 hours of hunger striking because the nature of his protest did not fall under the *totaal weigeraar* rules: HE WAS AGAINST MILITARY SERVICE, BUT WAS NOT AN ANTI-MILITARIST. Women were (and still are) accepted in the service on a volunteer basis only, and in this capacity were often ridiculed by the general public. Presumably, some were protesting for the right of compulsory service, or refusal; basically . . .

. . . to have the right to go to prison for not wanting to do something they are currently not required to do.

The subject of effectiveness of the Dutch armed services as a deterrent to potential enemies is an interesting one. One 1992 study indicated that about 30% of a military medical unit in Germany were registered drug users (the unit being known as the *"Military Hash Home"*). Hash, marijuana, cocaine and XTC were openly used throughout the military complex -- not a good basis for defending one's homeland.

Given that the purpose of a national army, navy and air force in western Europe is to maintain efficient, co-ordinated and fighting forces under the umbrella of NATO, only the Dutch could employ a Minister for Defence who strives to eliminate violence in the military and who is required to provide "relaxation advice" counseling for the troops. Apparently there is too much boredom and idleness in the Dutch barracks.

Why do they need this military "deterrent" anyway? In the words of Socialist Member of Parliament Klaas de Vries,

> *This is a self-regulatory society; it is not governed by speeches from above. We allow as many people as possible to be themselves. Some call that anarchy; we call it civilization.*

A spin-off advantage to involvement in NATO at least allows the Dutch image to be stressed abroad. The 1991 International Air Tattoo at RAF Fairford, England, featured a "Tiger Meet" as its main theme. The theme was chosen

The military deterrent

to celebrate the 30th anniversary of the NATO Tiger Association. Holland was one of 16 countries that took part. Their F-16 ground crew carried the tiger theme from head to toe, with safari hats and yellow-and-black striped wooden shoes.

(For more on the Dutch image abroad, see Chapter 19.)

Holland is a cheap place to live,
as the shops are always shut.
John G. Deacon, British Expatriot.

chapter 12

RULES FOR SHOPPING

T he Dutch love to window shop and to browse while dreaming of the ultimate bargain. Perhaps in fear of relenting to sales-pressure, many also suffer from the bizarre affliction known as ***drempelvrees*** (threshold phobia -- fear of entering shops, restaurants, etc.). Having managed to cross the ***drempel***, they revert to type. For your own protection, take heed of the following:

General

1. For smokers, before entering a shop, find a waste bin containing dry, combustible material in which to throw your burning cigarette.

2. When entering stores, let the door slam in the face of the person behind you. If you hear a loud thump or bang caused by a person in a cast, a pram or a wheelchair, nonchalantly turn around and mumble, *"Surrey whore"* (see Chapter 16). If you're in a particularly benevolent mood, you can further announce that you didn't notice the person's cast or wheelchair.

3. If someone gets in your way, place your hands on his/her shoulders and impatiently push the person aside as you show off your French, uttering, *"Pardon."*

4. If your purchases amount to less than HFl 20- and a queue of more than three people is formed behind you, pay by cheque or credit card and take at least five minutes to search for your identification. Alternatively, delay the transaction, using whatever means possible until the queue has extended to eight people.

5. Hunt for bargains and complain about prices of ALL produce/merchandise (see Chapter 8).

In Supermarkets

1. Take a few one-guilder pieces as deposit for use of a trolley. Until 1988/89 the peel-off ring-tab from a beer or soft drink can was considered by

much of the population to be legal tender for this purpose.

2. If a *cloggy* offers you an empty trolley in exchange for a guilder, beware! Either the mechanism for refunding your guilder is broken, or the wheels malfunction.

   Conversely, if you are the one with an empty trolley, never abandon it. In pouring rain, gale, hail, sleet or snow, you must return it to collect your investment – one guilder. Failure to do so will immediately brand you as a dumb foreign tourist who has no idea of the real world.

   If you find you simply must abandon it, get out of the way as quickly as possible. You may be crushed in the rush to redeem it.

3. Frequently block aisles with trolley.

4. Recruit kids to covertly load other customers' trolleys with expensive items.

5. At the check-out, the cashier must make two announcements: ***dag!*** and ***zegels?*** *Dag* means "good-day" and *zegels* means "savings stamps." The latter is NOT a guttural *Sieg Heil*, as many Germans have learned to their cost.

6. Check egg cartons for quantity and condition of contents. At least one egg will usually be broken or missing. Note also the "Dutch dozen" (***dozijn***): 1/2 ***dozijn*** = 6; 1 ***dozijn*** = 10.

7. Prod and poke delicate items. When about to leave, complain to the shop assistant about the poor quality of the produce.

8. Place little faith in barcode scanners and the like at the check-out. Review your receipt for errors before leaving the supermarket. If you don't, you may well come away unaware that the price reductions which attracted you in the first place were never applied.

Statiegeld and Borgsom

Statiegeld is the word applied to deposits on beverage containers. A beer bottle has a certain *statiegeld* value; a full crate has the quantity value plus some extra for the plastic container.

In a well publicized incident, a Dutchman lifted a quantity of bottled refreshments from a shop. He immediately deposited them in the store's recycling machine, thereby destroying the evidence of his crime and was duly rewarded for his environmental efforts in cash.

For discarding glassware with no value, there are recycling bins on street corners: one for coloured glass and one for clear glass. You may have to wait your turn to use these bins since it requires some studying before throwing bottles away. The owners want to make sure first that they don't ruin themselves financially by inadvertently throwing away a bottle for which they paid *statiegeld*.

At the time of writing, *statiegeld* is in danger of becoming extinct. Shopkeepers find the whole process too time-consuming, space-consuming and expensive(!) and want the system eliminated. The irony here is that the scheme was originally introduced not so much as a recycling effort, but more as a marketing ploy to attract customers. With coins being "reimpursed," the idea was an immediate success with customers, and a typical supermarket now finds it has to sort recyclable containers into 70 different crates and 90 different pallets. Much to the retailers' delight, studies are now underway to determine whether recyclable packaging or disposable packaging is better for the environment! Add to this the increasing black market in *"statiegeld*ed" containers (some shopkeepers build expensive high fences to protect their stocks of used bottles) and the whole thing seems doomed. (For more on recycling, see Chapter 15.)

Borgsom is similar, but is applied to video camera rentals, safe keys, Bicycle rentals, etc. Anything that will make it, they'll take it – and sometimes they'll fight you tooth and nail not to reimburse it.

If you are not sure if you are paying **borgsom** on a transaction, a good indicator is when the vendor asks you for some *legitimatie* (see Chapter 10) -- although it is unclear why a vendor needs proof of identity in order to borrow a few guilders from you.

We strongly doubt that **borgsom** will be threatened with commercial extinction in the foreseeable future.

Shopping for Clothes

1. When visiting fashion shops, take ear defenders with you to avoid permanent ear damage from the compulsory disco music blaring incessantly therein.

2. If you notice someone searching through a full rack of clothes, stand nearby and push the clothing apart so that you close the gap the person has made.

3. Take your children and encourage them to play hide-and-seek amongst garment rails.

At Street and Flea Markets

1. If you see an item you wish to buy, show minimal interest in it. Tell the vendor you saw the same thing for less than half the price at another stall in order to launch into a healthy bartering session.

2. If a crowd has gathered around a particular stall, push into the crowd, dig your elbows into those in front of you and breathe heavily in their ears to give them the hint to move out of your way. Conversely, if you are in the front row of a crowd studying the display of a stall and others try to elbow their way in, hold the fort. Do not leave until the crowd has dissipated.

3. When the market is extremely busy, walk against the flow of traffic, stopping frequently for no particular purpose.

chapter 13

DRIVING

As with shopping (see Chapter 12), a first experience of driving in Holland can be positively bewildering. But do not be dismayed. You are not an inferior driver. You have simply missed some elementary unwritten rules of the road.

Freewheeling Ways

1. Drive as close to the car in front of you as possible.

2. Change lanes constantly while driving. Roads are built from taxpayers' money. If you've paid your

taxes, it's your right to use as much of YOUR road as possible.

3. At least two cars should go through each red light. Avoid, at all cost, reducing speed or stopping. Any brake-light indication combined with an amber or recently-red traffic signal will subject you to a barrage of stereophonic horn-blasting even though it is considered vulgar to use the car horn except in an emergency.

WARNING: Beware of elderly drivers. They stubbornly adhere to the old-fashioned system of preparing to stop when the lights turn amber, and religiously stop at red lights. These senior citizens are the cause of many collisions.

---

4. If you witness a motorist driving through a red light, sound your horn violently in tribute while you visually scold the violator for his flagrant disrespect of the law.
Move alongside him and pound your head with your right hand. Appropriate angry facial expressions, bouncing up and down on your seat. Yelling *idioot!* (idiot), *godverdomme!* (God be damned) and *klootzak!* (scrotum) are beneficial. Never mind the fact that you are more of a traffic hazard than he was as you accelerate, slow down and wander across the fast lane, concentrating on your gesticulating.

5. If you are the first car to stop at a red light, do not expect to be able to see the traffic lights. Thanks to brilliant Dutch engineering, your car will be sitting directly under the lights. Just relax and rely on a honk or two from the car(s) behind you. Horns are guaranteed to sound if you do not react instantly to the green light.

Alternatively, step out of your car until the light changes. This at best is taken as a display of protest by the locals, and at worse is taken as an expression of your individuality. Both earn you much respect.

Road Rights

Dutch democracy on the road is exemplified by inconsistent yield signs, well described by the saying:

Sometimes the small roads have to have the power.

There would appear to be no general rule such as "priority to the right" or "priority to the main road."

Consider roundabouts as an example. In some places, the car coming from the right has the right of way. In other places, the car on the roundabout has the right of way. Elsewhere, traffic lights are used.

As local respect for speed limits is non-existent, popular means to slow down the traffic in residential areas include one-way streets and *drempels* (berms, or speed bumps).

Revised traffic laws (introduced in 1991) supposedly gave drivers more responsibility by reducing the number of rules to be followed. A *"rule of thumb"* was proclaimed: GIVE PRIORITY TO YOUR INTELLECT (which perhaps explains why no one gives way in traffic). Why such a fuss? The answer may lie in the list of Dutch notables caught in the act of committing driving offences that year, including:

- members of the royal family (again)
- the Prime Minister and members of his Cabinet, including the Minister of Defence
- Chairman of the Council for Traffic Safety.

The latter expressed much indignation at receiving a ticket for driving at 160 km/h (104 mph), declaring that it was a *"witch hunt for high officials who drive too fast."*

Traffic Jams

Traffic jams *(files)* are a frustrating experience in any country. In Holland, the feeling is worse with the realization that the 100 km (65 mile) line of stationary vehicles would more than span the width of the country.

What is unique is the wealth and extent of studies, proposals and laws generated to reduce them. When it was established that those selfish people who enjoy horse riding cause some jams, a law was passed requiring the horse (not its rider) to wear licence plates on either side of its head -- a sure way to improve traffic flow.

The studies, proposals and laws certainly made a difference. In 1994, a new national traffic jam record was set: on February 23rd, there were 43 traffic jams and 530 collisions, totalling 360 km (234 miles) of fuming, honking, clogged *cloggies*.

Getting Your Licence

There are two ways to obtain a Dutch licence: by taking lessons through an authorized driving school (*rijschool*) or by surrendering a valid foreign licence for a Dutch one.

The *rijschool* is rigorous and expensive, with rates at about HFl 2,000- to prepare you for your first driving test. All manner of interesting and unique equipment is used; some classrooms provide individual steering wheels and gear levers for the simulation phase. Do not be discouraged if you fail several driving tests; each additional course will only cost you roughly half as much again. And how good is the tuition? 30% of driving instructors give lessons without wearing a seat belt; with an average of 30 lessons required before taking the test, only 40% of driving students pass on their first attempt (1992). Strangely, the high cost of driving lessons has not been affected by protest (see Chapter 11).

Not all foreign licences can be surrendered for a Dutch one. Until the 1970's, most foreign licences were acceptable. Many Dutch would go to, for example, Egypt to obtain their licence. The total cost of the trip (including the licence) was less than the Dutch *rijschool* fees. In other words, the *cloggies* got a free vacation trip in the deal.

Now a foreign licence cannot be exchanged for a Dutch one unless the bearer can prove that he/she lived or worked in the foreign country for at least six months.

As Dutch territories (immune from the classification "foreign") were an exception to this rule for many years, places such as the Netherlands Antilles soon became the new favourites for obtaining licences. 1991 statistics showed more than 2,000 new Netherlands Antilles licences issued to residents of Holland were exchanged for the "real thing" when the newly-inducted motorists returned home. In the previous year, this figure was 500.

The Antillean island of Saba has freely admitted that its economy was directly dependent upon the *rijschool* trade. Tourism income (stemming mainly from this) was around HFl 500,000 per year, with an island population of approx. 1,000. Dutch students for driving lessons were recruited at the rate of 60 per week. As 1992 came to a close, so did this convenient method. Licences now are issued in the Netherlands Antilles only if six-month residency and other conditions are met.

There is one final route: join an experiment. Transport tutelage is a popular target for social experimentation, especially when combined with minority-group involvement. Look for programmes along the lines of this 1992 scheme:

> In an effort to help reform problem boys, some 30 Moroccan, Surinamese, Antillean and Turkish boys received a three-week crash course in driving at an army camp near Hilversum in order to get their licences. The goal was to prevent them from a "negative spiral" of crime. The driver's licence was to make it easier for each of them to find a job.

A once-thriving rijschool in Curaçao

*All hail the Dutch, long-suffering neutrons in the
endless movement against oppression and
exploitation. Let us hear it for the Dutch, bland
and obliging victims of innumerable wars
which have rendered their land as flat as their
treats. Every one of them is an uncle, not a one
can muster real courage. All hail the Dutch,
nonpeople in the people's war!*
Tony Hendra, National Lampoon, 1976

chapter 14

ON DUTCH CUSTOMS

Non-racist Nation

The Dutch boast that they are a non-racist nation. In the
1960's, the Dutch were extremely proud of the lack of
prejudice and racial problems in Holland (although in the
1940's the first Indonesian immigrants were looked down
upon as second-class people). But there was a reason for
this situation: non-Caucasians were a rarity in Holland in
those days. The result was that darker-skinned people were
idolized by the Dutch.

Things changed when Suriname became independent, and hoards of Surinamese flooded the country. The crime rate, drug abuse and number of people on welfare increased phenomenally. Immigration procedures soon tightened for dark-skinned applicants, hence, *"We support your cause, we appreciate your dilemma, but don't want you here."* Or, in the words of Dr. H. G. Boswijk, an Amsterdam clergyman, *"When Surinamers come to our churches, people observe a friendly distance. They say, YOU ARE WELCOME BUT LEAVE US ALONE. It's a kind of implicit apartheid."*

Yet, as soon as a resident visa has been issued, the Surinamese and other dark-complexioned immigrants (such as Turks and Moroccans) become a welcome part of the Dutch heart-throb, for they are now THEIR ethnic minority. In addition, they are on equal footing with the locals since they are eligible for welfare benefits.

And mankind must SEE that Holland leads the world in acceptance of other races in a western state. This attitude is demonstrated in the current policy of recruitment for the police force. One goal was to have a force consisting of 25% women and 10% minorities by 1990. In order to achieve this, a policy was established for Dutch citizenship to be granted in six months, instead of ten years, to successful applicants.

Even so, the evidence of discrimination persists, confirmed by muted governmental admissions, as the following examples show:

- Quote from the Mayor of Lelystad, 1991: *"Many immigrants come from countries where little or no culture exists. If they bring anything with them, it is their bad habits."*
- Employment agencies fill most job vacancies by bowing to racist demands from employers, de-

spite a 1987 code of conduct forbidding hiring of labour by discrimination. To substantiate these findings, the Ministry of Social Affairs commissioned the State University of Leiden to investigate the matter. Result? Case proved 90% of the time, using a study base of 134 agencies.

- In 1991, the Government Information Service conceded that it had researched the possibility of compiling "ethnicity facts" on gypsies, refugees, etc. If brought into law, such people would have to reveal to the authorities: their race, their parents' race and other such details.

To further fertilize their insistence that they are inherently non-racist, several governmental (and other) offices provide information, brochures and hot line services in the Moroccan and Turkish languages, whereas none of the same exist in neighbouring European languages. This is one of Holland's most useful contributions to the European Community.

In this complex era of racial-sensitivity issues, personal freedom issues, sexual liberation and killer disease, one trait remains an enviable quality of the Dutch. Black and white, friend and foe, male and female – all have an equal voice in the maelstrom of entitlement. White can always call "RACISM" against black without being called "RACIST" for doing so. Heterosexual can always call "DISCRIMINATION" against homosexual without the fear of being labeled "INSENSITIVE." All are guaranteed a forum. Much of the western world could learn an important lesson from them.

Manners Maketh Man

Little can be said about Dutch manners. *Cloggies* firmly believe their manners are impeccable, but to an aware foreigner they are as rare as a dike-mender's drill.

When abroad, *cloggies* assume no one they meet will speak Dutch. They ridicule others by making sarcastic and derogatory comments about them in Dutch. Occasionally they find themselves ridiculing fellow *cloggies*. No embarrassment or bad feeling ensues as:

- Both parties realize that they are guilty of the same.
- On discovery of their common nationality, both parties will agree that the ridicule is justifiably applied to the intended alien targets.

At home or abroad, a proper Dutch greeting consists of a brief handshake in the case of new acquaintances, or of a kiss on left-right-left cheek (= 3 kisses, total) for longer-term friends. These actions can be abbreviated, prolonged or combined, and apply to male-female and female-female greetings (not male-male, yet). Never misinterpret these rituals. Two women engaged in a handshake-1.5-kiss greeting does not signify a re-acquaintance between two lesbians who don't trust each other – it could well indicate that there are more important things to discuss. Whichever form/combination of greeting is used, it is often accompanied by a feeling of dread, as it gives rise to yet another national phobia: the fear of sweaty hands *(zweethanden)*.

Although a look of fear may at first be interpreted as mistrust of character, it is no cause for worry on the part of the sweat-recipient. Oddly, in 1991 a quarter of the Dutch population in the age group 18–50 were of the belief that AIDS can be contracted from a handshake – the sweatier the hand, the more chance of getting it. Thus, the sweatier the hand becomes, the higher the level of fear.

Correct adoption of parting gestures is as important as greetings. When leaving a friend's home at any time of day or night, stand outside the door and repeatedly scream *"daaaag"* at the top of your lungs. Then hop on your Bike and continue the serenade for a block or two. If your mode of transport is by car, drive off slowly, shouting *"tuuuuut"* as often as possible. Then speed up, making sure that the whole street knows that you have spent a lovely (in most cases, read "mediocre" or "boring") evening at your friend's home and that you are now leaving.

Another very common, affectionate way to say good-bye is to yell *doei* (pronounced *"doo-eee"*) several times. This expression is apparently used by the lower class, and is considered to be vulgar, stupid and a sign of lack of education.

Camping

Camping is a popular recreational pursuit. It is easy in Holland – official campgrounds are havens of comfort, with hot showers, shops, etc. Individual sites are marked, pre-planned by the owner, and there are obviously no "rough spots" on hillsides, etc.

Almost every household owns a camping shelter of some description. It can be a 1–2 person ridge tent, a grand family tent with awning and rooms, a caravan or a trailer. Yet not all are used for overnight accommodation. For some curious reason, *cloggies* make a habit of erecting tents in public parks for a few hours during a sunny day (the practice is quaintly called "day camping"). It may take 2–3 hours to travel, pitch the tent(s) and arrange the accessories (collapsible chairs for seating, table for coffee paraphernalia, potted plants and/or flowers, etc.) for a mere 45 minutes relaxing with nature – but they do it. *En masse.* So much so, in fact, that a sub-culture of **bermtourists** has developed. This strain of day-camper purposely seeks out space close to major highways in order to calmly complain about the excessive traffic and its consequences prior to becoming part of the problem on the way home.

At home or abroad, overnight public campsites are an excellent place for the young *cloggies* to sadistically impose their freedom on others. Around dawn, the little ones like to begin to sing Dutch children's songs; for a while, their parents will not interfere with this exercise of freedom and national pride.

When the songs finally get on the parents' nerves, they gently tell their little darlings to hush. The children exercise perfect disobedience and carry on singing and shouting. Those *cloggy* kids who do not like to sing can find freedom of expression by talking in an obnoxiously loud voice.

Older children (up to 30 years of age) have their rights to freedom, too, and often express themselves by playing football through the campsite. Other great places for the kiddies to play football are restaurants, *cafés*, full car parks, golf courses and metro trains.

Another favourite pastime is cussing and breaking wind. Making fun of others is, of course, a must, accompanied by lots of very loud giggling and cackling.

Sign Language

To become an accepted member of Dutch society, we recommend you practice the following, preferably in private:

- Place hand parallel to ear, 3 inches from ear. Oscillate hand in a forward/aft direction at medium speed. This means "delicious" *(lekker)*.
- Make a double thumbs-up gesture with lateral pumping action from the elbows, whilst religiously chanting *OMSTERDOM!!* This means, *"I like where I live."*
- Spread fingers, palms uppermost, and extend forearms. Tilt head to one side as you emit a sound not unlike a sick cow: *Jaaaaa.* This means, *"I don't really believe you."*

See Chapter 13 for special sign language when driving.

On Marriage

A popular contemporary attitude of unmarried couples living together *(samen wonen)* is that they should have the same rights as married couples. If the boyfriend's father dies, his partner feels entitled to two days' paid holiday for the occasion, as is the case for married couples. In the early 1990's, living-together registries were introduced as an alternative marriage register for couples (including homosexuals) who have entered into a living-together contract in front of a notary public. The partners can be "married" in the public marriage room of their local Town Hall.

Living-apart-together is commonplace as it allows couples to have their own life most of the time, but also to be together and have a shared non-binding commitment. Above all, there are tax and welfare benefits . . .

For couples who do elect to marry, the obligatory Town Hall ceremony (church ceremonies are supplementary and optional) clearly defines the extent to which the partnership is to be taken . . .

Money under matrimony is money shared.

The controversial topic of clergy and wedlock has been understandably fierce in Holland. The attitude is summed up in a BBC television interview with a Dutch theological student in the 1970's:

Q: *How do you feel about the idea of a priest being able to marry?*
A: *No question at all. It's a question of the priest himself, and not of other people. When I want to be a priest and I want to be married; and the Pope, he wants a priest (who) is not married; I don't want to be a priest!*

Get the idea? More on the consequences later.

Women's liberation has drastically modified the accepted format of a marriage. Dutch women, with their over-stretched sense of fair play, have achieved what they see as a "more equal division of labour" through the practice of partial or total role reversal. The authorities indicate their approval by awarding the major tax concessions to the higher income partner – male or female – rather than the traditional method of assuming the man is the family "breadwinner."

The Coffee Cult

Cloggies run on coffee. They can exist on over-boiled potatoes and cabbage, but they run on coffee. Fresh Dutch coffee – grown in politically correct countries charging the lowest price for the best quality, but always roasted and packed in Holland. Custom-built vending machines brew it and discard the unsold liquid at timed intervals. The armed forces take it on NATO manœuvres in thermos flasks. Truck drivers and businessmen alike *en route* to other European countries gorge themselves with it before crossing the border and complain bitterly about foreign coffee, drinking as little as possible for the duration of their trip. On special occasions, some shops, including certain supermarkets, lure customers with free coffee at times. At main railway stations and in intercity trains, vendors patrol the platforms and corridors with coffee carts. In all fairness, Dutch coffee far excels its dishwater-style cousins, served in the U.K. and U.S. It is strong and distinctive in flavour.

In keeping with this endowment, for years the populace has been treated to annual coffee-rating tests, sponsored by various organizations, including the well-known magazine/publishing house of Elsevier. Each year, different blends are tasted by experts (apparently armed with digital thermometers, magnifying glasses and vomit bags) at locations around the country in order to establish the "cream of the drop" in the same way that France, Spain and Germany rate their wines. Here is an extract from the result of a 1989 coffee test conducted by the national daily newspaper, *Algemeen Dagblad:*

ESTABLISHMENT	OBSERVATION (temp °C)	REMARKS
De Tukker, ALMELO (trad. HFl 1.5)	Smell of French Fries prevents one from smelling coffee. Cheap mixture, not bilious. (68)	Every coffee shop gets what it deserves.
Artis Zoo, AMSTERDAM (trad. HFl 1.75)	A sour cup of coffee. Dirty cups. (70)	If the animals got the same care, that would be the end of the zoo!
Academisch Medisch Centrum, AMSTERDAM (espresso HFl 1.85)	Good honest espresso. New cup required when waitress dropped my change into the coffee. (70)	Quite an achievement!
Smits Road House BELGIUM-NL Border (trad. HFl 1.90)	Cup of bile. Sore throat coffee. Inferior product. Stomach ache!	Welcome back to Holland!
Konditorei Gouverneur BERGEN OP ZOOM (trad. HFl 1.90)	Great coffee served in beautiful china. Top class. Fine taste. (71)	People who love their business and take care of all aspects. First class!
Wegrestaurant v.d.Valk Oriental Palace, BREUKELEN (trad. HFl 2.00)	HORRIBLE! Undrinkable. Quality of mixture extremely poor. Dirty spoons, dirty brim on milk jug. Also cold. (57)	Rubbish, sir. Pure rubbish!
't Wapen van Delft DELFT (trad. HFl 2.50)	Absolute loser. Coffee tastes like chlorine. Four dirty cups. (72)	Stale lubricating oil.
Centraal Station DEN HAAG (trad. HFl 1.65)	Vulgar, bitter, rotten taste. Cheapest in existence. (70)	Cup of bile!
Hotel Restaurant Wienerhof DEN HELDER (trad. HFl 1.90)	Even the most callous expert is disgusted. The mud wants to come down your nose. How dare they! Puddle in saucer soaked sugar bag. (66)	Just dirt.
Ferryboat "Counter" (DEN HELDER–TEXEL) (trad. HFl 1.70)	Black: practically undrinkable. With sugar: just syrup. With milk + sugar: lukewarm urine. (67)	Try tea.
Restaurant Bellevue, DORDRECHT (trad. HFl 2.50)	Strange aftertaste. Moldy? Ditch water? (67)	Do not despair. There are other shops around.

ESTABLISHMENT	OBSERVATION (temp °C)	REMARKS
Restaurant De Volder EINDHOVEN (espresso HFl 2,15)	Tired waitress drops cups on table. Pure and honest. (74)	Satisfactory.
Freddy's Snackcorner ENSCHEDE (trad. HFl 1.75)	Old coffee, absolutely unsuitable for consumption. (74)	Why is nobody protesting? How can this be ...!
Cafe de Drie Gezusters GRONINGEN (trad. HFl 2.0)	Sorry, no beating around the bush. A dirty, filthy cup of downright rotten coffee. A shock to your heart. (63)	Is there a doctor in the house?
Postiljon Motel HEERENVEEN (trad. HFl 2.25)	Just bearable. Personnel evidently in bad mood because it's another workday. (72)	One cup in the morning wakes you up screaming.
Cafe Hart van Brabant, 's-HERTOGENBOSCH (trad. HFl 1.50)	Bad, uninteresting, dirty. Inferior mixture. (71)	Would the proprietor himself taste the coffee which he dares to serve to his customers?
Eethuisje De Gordiaane LELYSTAD (trad. HFl 1.75)	Good blend, served with care but temp. differences. Sharp. (65-76)	Machine needs service. Good overall quality.
Engels, ROTTERDAM (trad. HFl 2.15)	Characterless coffee without aroma. Weak extract from poor mixture. Two dirty cups, spoons filthy, rings around milk jug. At first, change from waitress was HFl 75.00 short.	Why, oh why? It's about time somebody took care of this!
Restaurant Warenhuis Termeulen ROTTERDAM (trad. HFl 1.40)	No aroma, stench instead. Simply dirty. Murdered coffee. (72)	My stomach revolts. In need of fresh air before I vomit.
Coffeeshop Drinky Met, UTRECHT (espresso HFl 2.25)	Disinfectant? Chemicals? Salt? Dirty aftertaste. Undrinkable. (77)	Horrible!
Bar Michiel de Ruyter VALKENBURG (Limburg) (espresso HFl 2.0)	Well-groomed, clean, excellent blend. Perfect coffee, served hot. (81)	Champion espresso! Congratulations!

With this in mind, it makes you wonder why the stuff is so popular.

The method of drinking Dutch coffee is an art in itself:

1. Check that all the necessary components are present: cup of piping hot coffee; dwarf-sized spoon or stirring stick; condensed or powdered milk; and sugar.

2. Support cup in one hand. If a saucer is provided, do not hold the cup, but grip the saucer as if it were a frisbee about to be thrown.

3. Add milk to cup to colour (optional).

4. Add sugar to cup to taste (optional).

5. Stir continuously until cool enough to drink. If you use sugar cubes, pound the lump until dissolved, then stir vigorously for the remainder of the cooling period. If you added milk and/or granulated sugar, alternate between clockwise and counterclockwise stirring. If you drink your coffee black, stir however you choose. The important thing is to stare hypnotically into the cup while you stir.

6. Remove stirring implement from cup. Tap wet end 2–4 times on the rim of the cup. This indicates to your colleagues that you have completed the stirring phase and are about to enter the drinking phase.

7. Return stirring implement to cup.

8. Hold cup with fingers and thumb diametrically opposed. (If a saucer is present, do not use the hand holding the frisbee.) If the cup has a handle, insert middle two fingers through the handle. Extend index finger upwards and across the cup to

clamp the stirring implement against the far end of the cup. This is important as it prevents the thing from entering your nose in step 9.

9. Raise cup to mouth and slurp loudly while drinking. After first slurp, announce *"lekkere koffie, hoor!"*

The Other Cult

The Dutch possess a proven respect for religion. Traditionally, the country is divided between the Catholic and Protestant faiths (reference books are contradictory about the exact ratio; apparently even the Dutch can't agree upon what they are). Whatever the divide, it is modified to roughly 100:1 for the customary sport of POPE-BASHING.

The origins of this appear to be the archaic policies of the Vatican in respect to contraception, abortion, divorce, clerical celibacy and acceptance of homosexuality, not to

mention, of course, women's ordination (*Vrouwen* priests)–
in short, fucking and females.

Irrespective of centuries of papal politics and policies,
the blame for everything is placed firmly on the shoulders
of Pope John Paul II.

It all came to a head in May 1985 when Public Enemy
No. 1 visited Holland as part of his altar-stop tour. The
warm welcome provided by the Netherlands consisted
mainly of street riots, demonstrations, protest pop songs
("Popie Jopie" was the best-selling record), satirical
comedy in schools and on national television, etc. The
regiment of slogan writers originated such absolute gems
as *POPE GO ROME; PAUS RAUS* (get out, Pope!);*PAUS ROT OP!*
(piss-off, Pope!); and . . .

The following Sunday, the Dutch were back in their
Catholic churches, praising the Lord. No large queues were
evident at the confession boxes.

There was no apparent shame or embarrassment. No
one, Royalty or commoner, condemned the rioting, and

Prime Minister Lubbers reflected, *"The Pope came here as a man higher than others. That is not The Dutch way."*

The Birthday Party

Birthday parties begin around 8 pm and are held at the home of the birthday boy/girl *(jarige)*. Be sure to bring flowers and a gift if you want to be invited again.

The event somewhat resembles an open house. After entering, you will be ushered into the living room which, for the occasion, will resemble a doctor's waiting room, with chairs arranged in a circle. On them will be seated an array of relatives interspersed with the odd friend and neighbour. The relatives will welcome you to what at first appears to be a group therapy session, with all the appeal thereof.

The welcoming ceremony consists of walking around the room and shaking hands with each person. For some unknown reason, the relatives will extend their congratulations to you, the guest -- then mutter their name unintelligibly. Normal etiquette allows for this so that should you have the opportunity to enter into forced conversation with the person later on, you can always reopen the chat by asking for the name again.

Just when you feel you cannot put on another false smile, the tension will be alleviated by the entrance of coffee and cake. You should now join in with the echoed expressions of ecstasy, enthusiastically exclaiming to no one in particular, *"Lekker!"*

The atmosphere generally loosens up a little between cups, and people may rave about the lovely birthday gifts on display, about a course they are taking or about a recently acquired bargain. During this enlightening and captivating conversation, you will have ample opportunity to compile your next day's shopping list.

Coffee and cake consumed, round two invariably commences with beer or soft drinks, a few savouries and more conversation. This is your cue to evacuate your chair and socialize further afield. You can always retreat to the toilet or bring a premature end to a conversation that's become too overwhelming by spilling the remains of your coffee, beer or soft drink.

At some point, the conversation will be broken off for a round of *"Happy Birthday"* (in English) and/or the unfortunate Dutch equivalent which appears to be entitled *"In de gloria," "Lang zal Hij leven"* or *"Verjaars-lied."* (The absence of an official title for the song illustrates the national shame and embarrassment at such idiotic lyrics.) The singing is followed by a number of "hip hip hurrah's" as everyone appears to be having the time of their life.

When you feel the evening has reached its climax, or else any time between 10 and 11:30 pm, you may mark your departure by moving around the room once more to shake each person's hand again, mumbling goodbye and flashing your smile yet again.

CAN'T WAIT FOR THE NEXT ONE.

Other Festive Occasions

Queen's official birthday. This is celebrated 30 April (birthday of her mother) when there is some chance of dry weather, since the ruling monarch's true birthday is in January when the weather is guaranteed to be inclement. Many cities turn into a large flea market for the occasion. The Dutch save up their old junk and try desperately to sell it on this day. There are infinite street stalls, selling all types of food and beverage, spread throughout the town centre. The crowds are as unbearable as the overpopulated bars. There are flower parades, jazz and rock 'n roll bands, magicians, school marching bands and other unforgettable forms of entertainment.

Two Christmases. On 21st November, the Dutch Santa Claus *(Sinterklaas)* travels from Spain to Amsterdam by ship. After clearing customs (parking fines, excess toys, etc.), he is often greeted by the Queen before stocking-up with drugs. Santa has a white beard, wears a long red robe and tall red/gold hat and carries a golden crook. He is attended by his black manservant Black Peter *(Zwarte Piet)*, provided the former can prove that Peter is not his slave, and the latter can provide evidence that his presence is only temporary and dependent upon Santa's acceptance.

Traditionally, the Dutch celebrate Christmas *(Kerstmis)* on 5th December and again on Christmas Day/boxing day. There are two Christmases in order to split the material one (gifts) from the spiritual.

Gifts are exchanged on the 5th in celebration of the birthday of *Sint Nicolaas*. At night, children place their shoes by the fireplace. The shoes are filled with surprises from Santa during the night, which partly explains why Netherlanders have such big feet. Another tradition consists of "creating" and exchanging prank gifts. Each of these presents is accompanied by a silly poem (the more embarrassing the better) about the recipient. The "giver" understandably strives to remain anonymous.

Alas, there is strong evidence that the Dutch dual Christmas is on the decline. An increasing number of households are integrating the two events into one big

bash on 25th December (how original). The obvious financial advantage of this merger is subtly disguised as a
child-friendly manœuvre to protect against "Sint-stress." It
is claimed that the ranks of Dutch *Wunderkind* suffer stress
and trauma due to over-excitement and anticipation of the
Santa experience. Just how this stress is relieved by a
20-day delay is not abundantly clear.

New Year's Eve. As this is the only time fireworks are
allowed, it must follow that the Dutch New Year's Eve lasts
from 15 December to 15 February. Or do they celebrate
Blitzkrieg during this period? Your first experience of New
Year's Eve in Holland may give the distinct impression that
the country has gone to war. It is dangerous to walk about
town after 10 pm as the *cloggies* love to throw exploding
firecrackers at passers-by. This form of entertainment continues throughout the night. Bars and restaurants close at
8 pm and open again around 11 pm or midnight. Public
transport stops at around 8 pm.

Liberation Day. Traditionally, Liberation Day cel-
ebrates the freeing of the country from its Teutonic military
oppressors in 1945. Celebrations are now confined to
bashes every five years due to prohibitive costs. In actual
fact, the *Reichsmark* has been replaced by the *Deutschmark,*
soldiers have become tourists, and once again Wagner is
more popular than . . . .

National Windmill Day. National Windmill Day is not
observed nationally. Of all the areas that do observe it,
most do so in May. Presumably, most of the "most" have
windmills.

What wounds one's feelings in Holland is the perpetual consciousness that the country has no business being there at all. You see it all below the level of the water, soppy, hideous and artificial.
Matthew Arnold, 1859

chapter 15

BIKES, DIKES, FLAGS & FAGS

This chapter focuses on some traditional and contemporary things for which the Dutch have received a measure of global recognition. The list is understandably short and is headed by the tourist money-spinners: windmills and tulips -- both of which occur and recur in other chapters of this work. Here we include BIKES (in honour of Dutch perseverance with the infernal machines); DIKES (those all-important irrigation features, without which this book would be a collection of blank pages); royalty and patriotism (those ancient traditions that the Dutch simultaneously love and hate, typified by the practice of flying FLAGS at every slightest excuse); and homosexuals (coloquially referred to as FAGS in English-speaking countries).

Bikes

There are more than 15 million of them in Holland, and more than 600,000 of them in Amsterdam alone. They are multiplying at the rate of about 15% annually. Whether this only counts roadworthy vehicles or includes the mangled, decimated lumps of rusty no-wheelers chained to bridges and lampposts throughout the city is unclear. What is clear, however, is that the Dutch are SO fond of them that about 85% of the population BUY them, and some 4,500 miles (10,000 km) of dedicated paths honour them. They come in various shapes, sizes and vintage – irrespective of which, they are all dearly loved and respected. There is a thriving black market industry in them, and facilities for spares and repairs are almost as plentiful as dog *shit* on the pavements.

They are called *fiets* (pl, *fietsen*), probably because that's what powers them. Their drivers are Kings/Queens of the Road (Queen Juliana would ride one to the local street market) whose wanton disregard for other road-users encourages them to careen from kerb to kerb, up to four abreast.

Public buildings, parking facilities and public service vehicles are all designed with the two-wheeled wonders in mind. Most major roads (except highways) include a personal lane for them. Whenever and wherever possible, this lane is a separate thoroughfare, complete with its own road signs and traffic lights.

1   HAND-KNITTED (OR PLO-STYLE) SCARF
2   STIRRUP PUMP (NOT TO BE LEFT ON BIKE)
3   PLASTIC CARRIER BAG (SUPERMARKET OR BOOKSHOP ISSUE).
    MAY ALSO BE CARRIED ON HANDLEBARS
4   TYPICAL CARGO
5   PASSENGER SEATING/FREIGHT COMPARTMENTS –
    MAX. LOAD 250 LB (112 KG)
6   SIZE 10 EMERGENCY BRAKING SYSTEM (2-CHANNEL)
7   ANTI-THEFT DEVICE. MAY ALSO BE WORN AROUND NECK,
    OR WRAPPED AROUND SADDLE SUPPORT, IF PREFERRED
8   DYNAMO-DRIVEN HEADLIGHT (PREFERABLY DENTED) –
    SHOULD NOT WORK
9   BUNCH OF DUTCHNESS
10 COLLECTION OF "BUTTONS" WITH TOPICAL MOTIFS (PEACE, LOVE,
    ANTI-NUCLEAR NONSENSE, ETC.)

Nedlanderthal Man

These magnificent machines are used in many roles: as personal limousine, goods vehicle, freight wagon and taxi, thanks mainly to a twisted tubular steel accessory – the carrier. The carrier carries crates, kids, cats and canines alike (special child seats can be installed at the front and rear of the frame, for larger families). In the absence of these household items, it provides a rear seat for one or more passengers (traditionally the girlfriend, boyfriend, wife, husband, friend, house plant – or any combination of these). Heavier cargo (pianos, cupboards, etc.) require the borrowing/rental/purchase of a *bakfiets*, a sturdy *fiets* modified to incorporate a large wooden box or platform at the front.

Recent advances in *cloggy* cycle-ogy include:

- a rear picnic chair (you can either unfold the chair while still attached to the rear carrier, or detach it and use its telescopic legs)
- battery-free lights that operate for up to four minutes after riding
- high-tech bells that ring longer than the traditional variety.

Predictably, the criminal element has not been blind to the possibilities of an attractive income from the resale of rustled rigs. The cream of Dutch technologists are busily engaged in protecting the freedom of this threatened species. The rate of 900,000 stolen specimens per year (1991) is expected to diminish with the phased introduction of uniformed *fiets* patrol teams and video cameras in special stalls.

The future of safe-cycling is assured by a generous HFl 200-million governmental programme which extends to "bunkers" consisting of revolving lockers which can only be accessed electronically (first introduced in Eind-hoven), and roofing over *fietspad* (cycle paths). Even the Dutch railway service has joined the game with promises of the BIKE SHELTER OF THE FUTURE –a *fiets*-lovers' paradise where old machines can be laid to rest inexpensively and expensive racing types can be stored in a private vault. Magnetic cards can be used to access them using PIN codes for owner identification purposes. Robot cranes may be employed in a form of valet parking service . . .

Now, if only it were possible to generate this amount of enthusiasm towards combating other forms of crime.

End of a life-cycle

Dikes

The Dutch have been building dikes, dams, ducts and ditches for about 800 years – and they still need more. They've been seriously messin' about with water for longer – and they've still got plenty left. They've tried to blow it away with windmills, pump it away with windmills, convert it to paper and flour with windmills; and have created a tourist industry in the process. The product of their labours is called the Dutch "landscape": a subaqueous plain, or (almost) dried-up seabed, which would completely disappear if the sea level rose by 60 feet (20 metres).

A typical *cloggy* stands some 18 hands high, the equivalent of 6 feet 2 inches or 1.88 metre – noticeably taller than the global average. In the event of a natural disaster, these lanky lowlanders can act as human periscopes and view their country as it was before man despoiled it.

Perhaps due to their inability to tame the raging waters, they have become experts and innovators of waterways and bridges. They have partitioned an area of the North Sea, formerly known as the Zuiderzee, into a freshwater lake and are currently reclaiming large areas of this. A motorway runs across the lengthy partition *(Afsluitdijk)*. The southern delta region (prone to periodic flooding) has been harnessed by a series of hydraulic dams. None of this could have been achieved without serious protest, debate, demonstrations and compromise.

In 1958, Parliament made positive moves to protect the country against flood disasters as a response to public disquiet following the devastating floods of 1953. In the late 1960's, protests were voiced about the project. The completion date of the last and most complicated part of the project was set for 1978. This was delayed due to protest and debate focusing on the barriers being "normally open" (to maintain the natural environment) or "normally closed" (to ensure the safety of the population at all times). In other words: plankton vs. people. Complete closure, for which contracts had already been awarded, was out of the question. The compromise called for the barrier to be kept open in normal circumstances, but to be closed during heavy storms. All-in-all, the project was delayed some eight years and cost 30% more than estimated, with HM Queen Beatrix officially opening the storm surge barrier in October 1986. The *New York Times* acknowledged the feat with the following quote from Louis van Gestern:

> *This will end the mythology of the dumb little Dutch boy with his stupid finger in the dike to save his country.*

Ever eager to profit from their talents, the Dutch have exported H_2O control technology to the extent of creating picturesque coastal landscapes in countries where a barren interface previously existed.

Back on the domestic front, the remaining water does have its uses. A primary mode of industrial transportation is the canal. Barges are more commonplace than articulated vehicles. In mid-wintertime, when the water becomes ice for a few weeks, nothing is wasted. Ice skates are donned by all from 2 to 102 years of age for a season of free travel -- for leisure, business, sports and fitness.

Flags I -- Patriot(ic) Games

With true originality, the national flag is the French *tricolore* turned sideways, that is, blue under white under red. It is displayed at every excuse by the patriotic. Some will argue that the Dutch flag pre-dates the French one by some 200 years, but the fact of the matter is that it took four centuries of debate and demonstration (until 1937) for the Dutch to officially agree on the complex design and colour scheme.

The post World War II period saw the Dutch in the forefront of the drive for a unified Europe. During this phase, patriotism declined and fewer flags flew. With the goal of unity a supposed reality, Dutch fervour has refocused on the fear of losing their national identity. Flag manufacturers are predicting record sales for the rest of the 20th century. If homeland sales start to flag, they can always cut 'em in half, turn 'em around and sell 'em in Paris on Bastille Day.

National events with royal connections are denoted by the introduction of a long, fraying strip of toilet paper or ribbon, stained orange, and known affectionately as *"oranje wimpel"* to its foster parents. This streamer is intended to flap and fly freely above the horizontal *tricolore*, but given the Dutch climate, it tends to wrap both itself and its partner around the flagpole in one soggy, saturated wad.

Holland is one of the few European countries which still retains a monarchy as a figurehead -- adored and well loved, despite the obligatory scandals and obscene levels of personal wealth. (The Dutch royal family is among the most wealthy in the world.) One of the Orange-Nassau family's claims to fame involved Prince Bernhard, husband of the retired royal favourite, Queen Juliana. Not content to live in luxury courtesy of the Dutch purse, he enjoyed the fruits of favour "donated" by American defence firms in order to enhance the quality of their products. As a result of this scandal, the ever popular Queen Juliana, in true Dutch fashion, threatened instant abdication if her husband were subjected to the embarrassment of a public trial. After an "investigation," the Government agreed to drop the matter, providing that Bernhard van Lockheed resign from all official duties.

Not wishing to be outdone in the protest stakes, the Current Couple set the scene for their inauguration by establishing a link with the German Nazi era through associations with the *Hitlerjugend* and the *Wehrmacht*. Love prevailed, and Claus von Amsberg became the prince consort of the Netherlands. At the regal betrothal (1966), some 1,000 *cloggies* violently demonstrated, shouting, *"Claus, raus!"* (Claus, get out!). It took 17 years for the Dutch to accept this latest Teutonic invasion, and then only so after the following:

- By Royal Decree and marriage, Claus von Amsburg was renamed HRH Claus George Willem Otto Frederik Geert, Prince of the Netherlands, Jonkheer van Amsberg.
- Willem-Alexander, the Crown Prince of the Netherlands was born -- the first male heir to the Dutch throne in more than 100 years.
- HRH suffered and recovered from a mental breakdown and severe bouts of depression (necessitating frequent travels to Italy to play golf).
- HRH was diagnosed with Parkinson's disease.

The process has now turned completely around, with the general public displaying much sympathy and (as close as they can get to) compassion for THEIR Claus.

The fact that the vast majority of the Dutch love to own a Royal Family may at first seem out of character for obviou$ reasons. As one royal supporter explains, *"As long as the royals are not too pretentious and talk sense, we don't mind supporting them. A president wouldn't be much cheaper --*

we have already calculated this!" The Queen is well respected for most of her activities, including an occasional
mingle with the masses by riding her Bike to the street
market or even (on at least one occasion) through the Red
Light district of Amsterdam. Her popularity has remained
at about 90% in the polls, with only 4% opposed to her.
Most citizens are also supportive of Crown Prince Willem-
Alexander and feel he will be well prepared to become King
by the turn of the century.

Flags II – Regal Rubbish (and its disposal)

As a further indication of Dutch latent belief in the divine
rights of royalty, all goods deposited on the streets are
officially the property of the Crown. If on royal-rubbish collection day your neatly bundled waste has not been
removed but stands solitary at the entrance to your abode,
the reason must be that either:

- Their Majesties have sufficient stocks of rotting
  kitchen waste, etc., to last until next collection
  day.
- You have been officially honoured by the Crown,
  who have decreed that you may keep that week's
  tribute as a royal bequest.

However, you have some possibilities concerning the
immediate problem . . .

1. Leave the rubbish where it is.
   City authorities will not notice your rubbish
   amongst the scattered heaps of monarchial
   mess.

The neighbours, however, will. They will probably write you a nasty note or come to your home and complain about their Queen's garbage YOU left on the street. Children, dogs, cats, birds and vermin will rip the sack open and spread the contents about (reaction from neighbours as above).
Rural authorities will notice your rubbish and will most likely take action against you.
2. Remove the rubbish to a skip, a rubbish heap or another street where the palace has yet to make its collection.
In cities, no one will care in the least. However, it is only fair to warn you that in the country, civil servants are a bored species and will inevitably search through the container(s), looking for clues of ownership. If the bag contains any items which include your name and address, you can expect to receive a photocopy of the evidence, along with a warning *(waarschuwing)*. After a second warning, you'll be reported to the police and/or fined, presumably for stockpiling stolen goods.

Oversize rubbish can be abandoned on city streets on collection day and will be collected by a special service. Oversize-rubbish-eve and -day provide a fascinating view of Holland as many streets are decorated with items such as refrigerators, stoves, washing machines, pianos and furniture. Understandably, many of these reusable items disappear from the street before the official collection service arrives.

In towns or villages, the local authorities are far more respectful of their Queen's property. You can make an appointment to have oversize rubbish collected once a fortnight. Bear this in mind on the day you buy your Christmas tree, as you should, on the same day, make an appointment to have it hauled away a few weeks later.

No discussion on rubbish collection can be complete without a mention of the Rampant Recycling Rage. The Dutch have long given up on using household refuse as a means of elevating their ground level and have embraced recycling with vigour – perhaps it was a misinterpretation of the term re-cycle-ing that started 'em off. Villages, towns and cities alike have embarked on various complex schemes in an attempt to out-recycle the rest.

Peter Spinks, a writer for *New Scientist* magazine, summed up the situation admirably in his exposé of the recycling effort in his adopted town of Egmond:[1]

> "Each household has a set of green and grey bins with black plastic wheels. They are emptied at bin stations, on alternate weeks, by a hulk of a yellow and red refuse truck with flashing lights and an automated bin lift. By the time the truck arrives the refuse has, in theory at least, been separated into recyclable parts. Vegetable peelings, uneaten food, plants and garden debris go in the green bin; plastics, metal, hardboard and the like go in the grey one. Glass bottles, which are not deposit-refundable, must be taken to the communal glass dumps. Newspapers and magazines are collected monthly, with luck, by schools; string, ribbon and old clothes are collected twice a year by the Salvation Army.
>
> For a start, paper collection, a dire necessity for newspaper-accumulating journalists like myself, requires the patience of Job and the logistics of a Stormin' Norman-style strategist. The schools,

1   This first appeared in New Scientist, London, the weekly review of science and technology.

which regard paper collection as less a profession than a charitable hobby, make their collections the first Wednesday of the month, unless that is a public holiday, in which case they collect on the second Wednesday. Neither advance warning nor a calendar of collections is given to households, who need to keep track of 'paper days.'

The bins, too, require constant attention. In winter, to loosen garbage frozen to the sides, householders are advised to place bins in the sun, if and when it shines. Come summer, the decomposing-contents of the green bins should be emptied, with noses pegged, into the grey bins, thus rubbishing the whole idea of separating refuse.

Not that the separation process itself is exactly straightforward. Take the supposedly simple tea-bag, for example. To be religious about it, as the largely Calvinist Dutch are about most things, the wet tea leaves should be removed from their filter-paper bag and deposited in the green bin. The bag, once ironed dry, should be put aside for the infamous paper collection, along with the tea label (after removing the metal staple, which goes in the grey bin) and the piece of string, which is rolled up for the Salvation Army.

To keep separators on their toes, compliance is monitored by a petty-minded bank of bin inspectors, who police the streets armed with indelible red pens. Their brief is unenviable but clear: to ferret around, elbow-deep, in bins whose owners can be identified by prominently displayed numerals indicating house numbers. The bins of first-time offenders are marked with warning crosses; those of second offenders, horror of horrors, are not emptied.

Transgressions are easier to detect in green bins. Therefore the rule of thumb is: when in doubt, go grey rather than green. This is what many Egmonders now do, even when not in doubt. The practice explains why fewer and fewer bins appear on 'green weeks' and why grey bins invariably overflow, leaving a smelly mixture of rubbish strewn across the once-spotless streets."

One wonders what the Queen has to say about this shambles.

Fags (and Fagettes)

Gay boys and gay men (*flikkers*) came out of the closet in the 1960's. The discovery of the fact that there were other *flikkers* about, fired by their inherent (Dutch) rebelliousness and permissiveness, led to the formation of *aktie* groups, followed by demonstrations, gay rights movements, gay centres, gay bars, hot lines and periodicals.

The inevitable reaction of **Vrouwen** homosexual movements took place soon thereafter, with lesbians demanding equal rights and more-than-equal facilities. Holland was one of the first (if not the first) to provide generous welfare benefits to a lesbian couple who "had" a child through artificial insemination.

Despite their common homosexual *raison d'être*, gays and lesbians are separate entities. In general, women are marginally accepted in gay bars while men are more taboo in lesbian bars and *cafés*. One area of commonality is that of self-glorification. The aptly-named newspaper *"De GAY Krant,"* in August 1988, listed gay and lesbian facilities in approximately 100 Dutch cities, towns and villages, including 180 entries for Amsterdam alone.

Amsterdam's liberal locals constructed the world's first monument to homosexuals in 1987 -- an obvious structure in the form of three large triangles, painted pink. Soon after, work started on a portable *homomonument* which was presented to the British Government as a protest against proposed anti-homosexual legislation. The rest of the population strives to be extra "open" and accepting of homosexuals, bisexuals and portable monuments.

Obtaining gay rights and gay acceptance in Holland has required less of a struggle than in most countries. The gays fought their battle according to Dutch rules: long and detailed discussions; non-violence; demonstrations; playful behaviour rather than being aggressive, obnoxious and pushy; and appealing to Dutch tolerance. In addition, many Netherlanders consider it a plus rather than an effeminate minus for men to be cultured and artistic -- traits often associated with the gay community.

Gay rights are part of a general pattern of rights for all groups that demand (and obtain) a place in Dutch society. This *verzuiling* phenomenon, whereby society is divided into pillars or blocs which are separate from each other yet support the society as a whole, has been very successful in the Netherlands. For the majority of homosexuals, the struggle is over and it's business as usual, even though the supposed tolerance for homosexuality is often superficial (especially in the countryside). A father who has a modern and tolerant view towards homosexuality may be terribly shocked to find out that his own son is moving about in homosexual circles. Some families console themselves with the excuse that it is fashionable to be gay. But recent research indicates that (some) gay males may be born with homosexual tendencies.

The last words on this subject must go to a Professor of Sociology in Groningen who proclaimed (in 1991) that the distinction between the sexes is disappearing. Apparently, a society in which androgyny and bisexuality are the norm is HEALTHIER AND SAFER FOR THE ENVIRONMENT. Sharing similar feelings and sexual relations with several people at one time is supposed to help solve problems of:

- loneliness (no kidding)
- economic over-consumption (?)
- war (tell that to a war widow(er))
- vandalism (too tired?)
- health care (tell this one to the thousands of AIDS victims in Holland).

---

*The Dutch language, in its written form, looks
like someone sat on a typewriter!*
The Dutch Courier, Australia

chapter 16

THE DUTCH
LANGUAGE

L ike most nationalities, the Dutch insist that their tongue
is a difficult one. It is the 6th language of Western
Europe and is spoken by some 30 million people worldwide.
This includes two very similar languages: Flemish (*Vlaams*)
in Belgium and Afrikaans in South Africa.

Dutch is basically a form of German which borrows
heavily from English and French, although most native
speakers will vehemently deny this. If you speak German,

you will have an easy time with Dutch. From a grammatical viewpoint, it is easier than German.

Dutch is rarely encountered abroad. Basically, there is no need for it outside of the country, especially since the Dutch are so proficient with languages. Conversely, if you spend more than half a year in Holland without learning the language, your Dutch acquaintances will appear offended that you have not learned their wonderful language.

If you take a course in the Dutch language and finally progress enough to dare to utter some sentences in public, the person you speak to will inevitably answer you in what they detect to be your native European tongue. They love to show off the fact that they have learned one or more other languages.

---

*The more you try to learn Dutch,
the more the Dutch refuse to speak
Dutch to you and the more they
complain that you haven't learned it.*

The abundant use of many vowels (including double vowels), as well as the construction of long words (as in German), gives the written language the appearance of being difficult. However, Dutch is very regular in its pronunciation and grammar.

Foreigners may be surprised to discover that several dialects are spoken within the borders of tiny Holland. They include **Gronings** (from Groningen), **Volendams** (from Volendam) and **Brabants** (from, believe it or not, Brabant). Lesser known (and lesser pronounceable) varieties include

Drents, Saksisch, Gelders and *Zeeuws*. There is also a separate language, *Fries,* in the northern province of Friesland.

Throat Disease (pronunciation)

There are only a few difficult sounds: the gutturals (represented by the letters *"ch"* and sometimes by *"g")*; the *ui, ij* or *ei*; and the single versus double *"a"* (*man, maan*). If you have never encountered the language but are tempted to experiment with these examples, try reciting the list of ingredients from a soup can, with your mouth half-full of syrup.

During World War II, the military's secret test of the Dutch nationality was to have an individual pronounce the name of the town of Scheveningen. Foreigners failed when they pronounced it along the lines of "Shave-a-Nigger." Imagine the outcome of "Groningen."

It takes some time for outsiders to grow accustomed to the sight and sound of the native's names, as they are long and numerous. Although you will probably be asked to use a one-syllable, vowel-happy forename (Huub, Jaap, Riet), the birth name is invariably a formal one, followed by 1–5 middle names and a surname. In the case of married women, the maiden name is attached with a hyphen.

Examples . . .

- Peter Johannes Theodorus Gustav Arnoldus de Jong
- Hubertus Cornelis Johann Maria van Dijk
- Wilhelmina Johanna Carola Petra Van Leeuwen-Waterdrinker.

For obvious reasons, the official combinations rarely appear anywhere except on larger legal documents.

Parents can decide if their children bear the last name of the mother or the father. If the parents are not married, a civil servant or registrar will decide which last name the child gets. This is an important decision since it is extremely difficult to have one's name changed in the country. Names are usually only changed by royal consent after a long process. The only exception is if the name is embarrassing.

Grammar

There are two genders: neuter and a combined masculine/feminine. The masculine-feminine merge (or noun "lib") happened years before gay- and women's "lib."

Nowadays there are three forms of "you." *U* is polite, formal and used in business and with elders. The use of this form of "you" shows respect. *U* is used less and less these days. If its use deteriorates in proportion to the national lack of respect, it will soon be extinct. Either *jij* or *je* can be used for the singular familiar form; *jullie* is the plural form (not a girl's name).

The character of a people is reflected in its language. An example of this is seen in the compulsive-obsessive use of diminutives in daily speech. As a Dutch physician explains, *"Everything has to bear the stamp of the small-scale complacency, which personally I consider to be one of our most typical features."*

The suffix *-je* is the most common way to exercise this. The Dutch drink *een kopje thee* (a little cup of tea), take little strolls *(gaan een straatje om)* and take little journeys around the world *(reisje om de wereld).*

Trend Setters

Hallo
Don't let what appears to be friendliness fool you when you first arrive in Holland. When someone says *hallo* to you, this is most likely not a greeting but rather an explicit expression of contempt to draw your attention to something stupid you have done. It is generally used to embarrass. This is most effective with non-Netherlanders.

Sorry
Common form of lip service, often used in combination with "whore," as in "Surrey whore" *(sorry, hoor).*

SVP
The French "silver plate" (spelled *s'il vous plaît*) is often used in its abbreviated form, *SVP*, on signs and in letters as a replacement for its direct Dutch equivalent *AUB* (in full, *als 't u blieft*) or *"(if you) please."*

Spelling Corruptions

Much of the population likes to use modern or progressive spellings which are not yet official, such as *buro* for *bureau* or *Odeklonje* for *eau de cologne*. The latter also exemplifies the battle between traditionalists, who prefer to leave *"c"* as *"c,"* and those who consider themselves progressive, preferring to replace a hard *"c"* with *"k."* This struggle is resolved in some dictionaries by a blanket statement, *"If not found here, look under "c" ("k")."*

Intrinsic Idioms

Predictably, Dutch idioms show an overall obsession with the three "W's" (windmills, wooden shoes and water), as well as flowers and Bicycles. Try these phrases out on your Dutch colleagues and take note of their reaction and facial expressions as you do.

WINDMILLS ...

een klap van de molen hebben
(lit., get hit by the windmill)

to be crazy

dat is koren op zijn molen
(lit., that is wheat to his mill)

a strong point of a person's argument

iemand door de molen halen
(lit., run someone through the mill)

to scrutinize someone's character

met molentjes lopen
(lit., walk with toy windmills)

to be silly

WOODEN SHOES ...

blijf met de klompen van 't ijs
(lit., keep your clogs off the ice)

keep out of it; mind your own business

met de klompen op het ijs komen
(lit., go on the ice with wooden shoes)

to butt in, rush headlong into business

Nou breekt mijn klomp!
(lit., now my clog breaks!)

Good Lord! What next?

op je klompen aanvoelen
(lit., feel it with your clogs)

to be obvious

WATER, CANALS, DITCHES, ETC. . . .

ouwe koeien uit de sloot halen
(lit., get old cows from the ditch)

to talk of things past

met de hakken over de sloot
(lit., with the heels over the ditch)

to make it by the skin of one's teeth

bang zich aan water te branden
(lit., afraid to be burned in water)

to be/become timid or fearful

zo vlug als water
(lit., as fast as water)

as fast as lightning

hij loopt in geen zeven sloten tegelijk
(lit., he doesn't walk in seven ditches simultaneously)

He can look after himself; no harm will come to him

aan de dijk zetten
(lit., place on the dike)

to dismiss, fire

water naar de zee dragen
(lit., carry water to the sea)

to perform unnecessary actions

(iemand) van de wal in de sloot helpen
(lit., help someone from shore into the ditch)

to make things worse

de druppel die de emmer doet overlopen
(lit., the drop that makes the bucket overflow)

the straw that broke the camel's back

het water staat mij tot de lippen
(lit., I am up to my lips in water)

I am up to my neck (in difficulties, etc.)

recht door zee gaan
(lit., go straight through the sea)

to be frank

spijkers zoeken op laag water
(lit., look for nails at ebb tide)

to find fault, nit-pick

FLOWERS . . .

de bloemetjes buiten zetten
(lit., put the little flowers outside)

to paint the town red

de bloemen staan op de ruiten
(lit., the flowers are standing on
the window panes)

the windows are frosted
over

iemand in de bloemetjes zetten
(lit., place someone in the little
flowers)

to treat someone like a
king/queen

BICYCLES . . .

doorfietsen
(lit., cycle through)

to flip or thumb through

voor elkaar fietsen
(lit., manage to cycle)

to wrangle, manage

ga fietsen stelen op de Dam
(lit., go steal bikes at Dam
Square)

Drop dead !

*wat heb ik nu aan mijn fiets
hangen?*
(lit., now what's hanging on
my bike?)

What kind of mess am I in
now?

chapter 17

FOOD FOR THOUGHT

culinary character

Some Traditional Dishes

The international respect bestowed upon the Dutch cuisine is reflected in the abundance of Dutch restaurants found in London, Paris, Berlin, New York or Baghdad.

Culinary orgasmic delights such as *stamppot* (mashed potato with cooked vegetables/meat/fruit stirred in – as the concoction is pounded almost into a pulp, nobody is quite

sure what the featured ingredient is) somehow do not en-
tice the gentry as do *coq au vin à la bourguignonne* or
scaloppeine di vitello al Marsala. And Edam **kaas** (cheese) is
no match for *Caprice des Dieux* or Swiss *Gruyère.*

Appelgebak (Dutch apple pie) differentiates itself from
other countries' traditional versions by the ritual around
which it is consumed. Preferably accompanied by close
friends in a *gezellig café*, the **appelgebak** (with or without
slagroom – whipped cream) and cups of fresh, hot coffee,
are slowly consumed, each mouthful garnished by deep
and meaningful social intercourse.

Erwtensoep is Holland's ceremonial centre-piece, succulent starter, majestic main course . . . whatever. It consists
of a delicious, thick pea soup infested with lumps of ham
and vegetable(s). It is served with spoon and bib and is
available in kit-form at specialist shops and in canned- and
powdered-form at supermarkets. It's as close as you can
get to a national dish – or national bowl.

Hutspot (mashed potato with onions, carrots and a sug-
gestion of meat, swimming in a rich gravy) is a hearty dish,
about as exciting as such a stew can be. It is most popular
in the winter months.

Uitsmijter (ham/cheese and two or three semi-fried eggs
on untoasted toast) is mainly adopted as a lunch time treat
when even the Dutch cannot face the standard fare (see
below).

There are, in general, little or no regional differences in
the way traditional dishes are prepared, although some
areas sport local traditional delicacies such as *Balkenbrei*
(North Brabant): flour, pigs' blood and lard, cooked and
served with fried bacon.

Midday Morsels

The standard lunch time *pièce de résistance* is a tantalizing choice between open- or closed-sandwiches. *Cloggy* bread, which is rather dry and bland to the point of seeming stale, is lightly smeared with unsalted butter or unsalted margarine and topped with translucent slithers of processed ham or processed cheese. The unsalted lubricant is probably an attempt to counteract the effect of the highly salted topping. (Edam cheese is salted during manufacture in order to give it a bit of taste.)

Their salt sandwiches are invariably eaten with a knife and fork, and are washed down with coffee or fruit juice to avoid dehydration.

The final course is typically one apple, pear or orange, peeled with the same knife that was used to dissect the main course. For an experience of poetry in motion, observe the way the Dutch peel their fruit:

- With apples and pears, a helical peel length is attempted: whether it is achieved or not is largely irrelevant, unless you are superstitious. It is the style of execution that matters. The (blunt) knife blade careens around the fruit from stalk to stub in a continuous, poetic, lethal motion – a combination of Marcel Marceau and Jack the Ripper. For the superstitious, tradition dictates that if you hold the peel above your head, then drop it, the shape of the peel that falls to the deck spells the initial(s) of the peeler's next lover. Apparently ours are GIU and SCUG.
- With oranges, the top (and possibly the bottom) is first circumcised. A surgical incision is then made at what is left of the stalk-end, and the knife

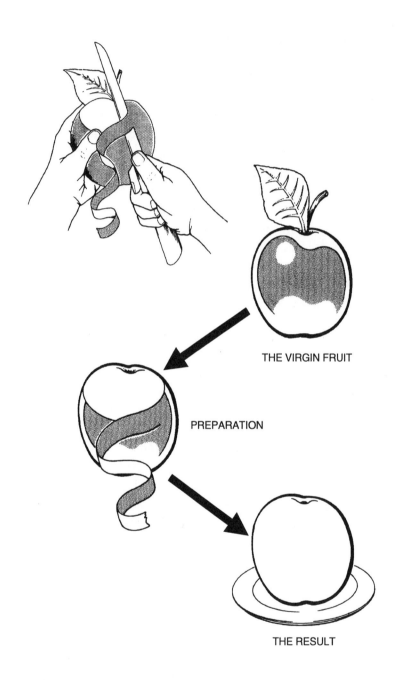

THE VIRGIN FRUIT

PREPARATION

THE RESULT

apples

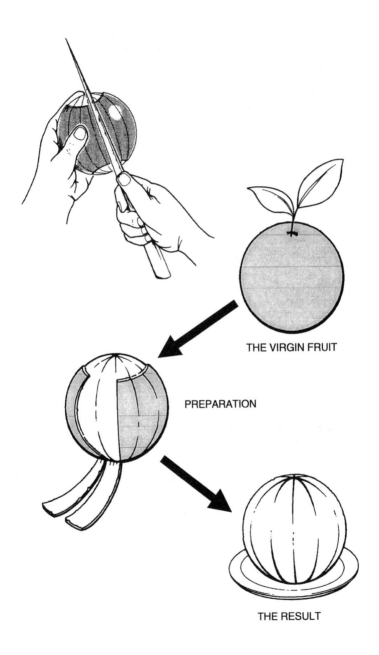

THE VIRGIN FRUIT

PREPARATION

THE RESULT

oranges

is drawn down to the ex-stub. Successive movements are made at roughly 30-degree intervals
to divide the peel into regular segments. This
done, the consumer manages, somehow, to split
all segments in turn, and the inner sanctum of
the deflowered fruit is laid naked for ingestion.

Consumption is secondary to the display of conquest,
as the frockless fruit lies helpless in the hands of the rapist,
like a British politician at a European monetary convention.

So from where does this exclusively Dutch characteristic
stem? The most rational and likely explanation is the
Dutch potato passion, the favourite recipe being whole,
boiled potatoes, known as *boiled potatoes*. There is only
one way to peel a cooked potato while keeping it intact
and that is to use the spiraling-down technique, in one
continuous stroke from the north- to the south-pole of the
potato. This style of skinning spuds subsequently spread
to the peeling of round fruits.

Restaurants

Foreign restaurants are popular social gathering points
in towns and cities. Italian, Greek, Chinese and Indonesian
eating establishments are commonplace. Turkish, Indian
and Mexican are breeding fast. Unfortunately, the dishes
served are often corrupted by substitutes for certain unob-
tainable original ingredients, as is the case in all European
countries.

Dutch traditional restaurants also exist. They serve
some or all of the dishes previously mentioned, and soup-
up the attraction by including other European classics,

such as *Wienerschnitzel, Jägerschnitzel,* steak (*biefstuk*) – child's portion – and *Tartar* (minced, raw steak, *tartaartje*).

More important than the food is the *ambiance* that permeates the place. Basically, the cosier the climate, the more popular the establishment. If the *milieu* is to their liking, the Dutch do not mind forking out a little more than usual. The incredible atmosphere of many of the restaurants is reflected in the overall *décor*, due to a *mélange* of all those wonderful and typical features touched upon in this work, such as flowers, plants, coffee, apple pie, cleanliness, music, friendliness of staff and price range. Lighting, furniture, architecture and style of dishware (porcelain, etc.) are also important. Political, religious, or "good cause" affiliations are often used to lure customers; in these eating houses, posters and propaganda flavour the scene.

Whatever the locale, there is a definite etiquette that is followed when the meal arrives. Before commencing your meal, wish your companion(s) *bon appétit* by uttering one of the following: *eet smakelijk, smakelijk eten* or *eet ze.* And observe the "paying protocol."

The "paying protocol" prescribes that if you are invited out for a meal, you pay for yourself ("go Dutch"). If someone else pays for your meal, reciprocate as soon as possible.

Snack Bars

Snack bars introduced themselves in Holland long before the concept of "fast food" infested western culture.

Banks of coin-operated hatches (*automaten*) set in walls announce the presence of gastronomic goodies such as over- or under-cooked chicken (*kip*) wings, hamburgers, potato croquettes *(kroketten)* and fascinating noodle slabs *(bami-bal)*. Together with the compulsory salted French Fries (swimming in mayonnaise), this type of convenient meal provides just the thing for a healthy jogger to feast on after a strenuous workout.

Perhaps more popular are the relatively new *shoarma* snack bars which identify themselves by the presence of a vertical grilling device (containing a rotary spit, heavily loaded with thin, wide slices of lamb) strategically located at the front of the ex-shop. These establishments assemble the Middle East version of hamburgers, consisting of dissected pita bread loaded with hackings from the spit, weeping green-salad components and a hot sauce, guaranteed to mask any natural flavour.

Tipp(le)ing

Most restaurants throughout Europe automatically include a 15 percent tip in the bill. Standard Dutch practice is to leave an additional coin or two on the table to express gratitude to the staff and thereby avoid appearing Dutch. That extra 10-cent tip is considered a tremendous token of appreciation by Dutch restaurant clientele. We doubt this sentiment is shared by the restaurant staff.

For those who prefer their sustenance in liquid form and a little stronger than milk, Dutch bars are also places of intense social discourse and atmosphere. Some are open 24 hours a day, some daytime only, some evenings/ nights.

If you drink alone, there is no chance of boredom as most bars provide a monumental display of curiosities and collections on their walls. If the bar has a history, you'll find it on the walls; if the owner has a history, you'll find it on the walls; if its name suggests a theme, you'll find it on the walls; and so on. If you find a bell hanging from a rope, or a rope hanging from a bell, don't ring it, despite possible encouragement from the locals. By doing so, you're agreeing to buy all present a drink of their choice. Be cautious when using the phrase, *"Let's have a drink"* (***borrel*** or ***borreltje***), as it can easily be interpreted as, *"The drinks are on me."*

Dutch gin *(**genever**)* can blow your head off. Dutch beer *(**bier; pils**)* is sweet, tasty and strong. Ordering a beer can be confusing for foreigners who attempt to do so for the first time in Dutch. No matter how you refer to a "beer" in Dutch, the bartender will respond by using a different term. Here, the obsession with diminutives (see Chapter 16) comes into play:

Mag ik een bier?	(May I have a beer?)
Een biertje?	(A beer? - lit., A little beer? doesn't refer to size)

Mag ik een pils?	(May I have a beer?)
Een pilsje?	(A beer? - lit., A little beer? doesn't refer to size)

For a small glass of beer, use the double diminutive:

Mag ik een kleintje pils?	(a small beer - lit., May I have a small little beer?)
Een kleintje?	(A small one? does refer to size)

Beer is generally served in small, flower-pot shaped glasses. When poured or pumped into these containers, a considerable amount of froth or "head" develops, which is sliced flush with the rim. The resultant offering often shocks European visitors. Germans laugh at the sawn-off "head" and protest the lack of quantity (as usual) while Brits laugh at the lack of quantity and protest the over-abundance of "head." French and Italians just drink it and think romantic thoughts of home, while Americans eye it with pity, demanding,

I'll have a low-cal, low-cholesterol, extra oat-bran, sugar-and salt-free beer with a twist of lemon – and gimmie some diet floss and decafeinated ketchup with that!

Dutch Sushi

Long before the western world discovered the intimate luxury of sitting at a low, black, lacquered table to feast on Japanese raw fish, the Dutch were doing it in quite another manner – and continue to do so in no lesser style. Standing in front of an open-air fish stall, ranks of cloggies hold raw, brine-slimed herring *(haring)* sprinkled with raw, diced on-ions in the air, and lower the ex-creatures into their gaping gates. Two swallows and a series of lip-smacks later, the onion debris is wiped from their mouths and clothing, and the feast is over.

A similarly repulsive practice exists with eel *(paling)*, the thin variety being smoked and the thick variety being fried or served in butter sauce. Here the vomit-buds are teased by the fact that the eel heads are left on for consumption at the more ethnic establishments.

Dutch Rusk

It's called **beschuit met muisjes**. Don't even try to pro-nounce it. It means something like DUTCH ENGLISH MUFFIN WITH BABY MICE, the **muisjes** being pink-and-white aniseed sprinkles. It is highly inadvisable to attempt to prepare

Harvesting haring

and/or consume this traditional snack without proper and thorough demonstration and instruction from a native.

Beschuit are round, extremely dry, light and very fragile biscuits. You cannot cut a *beschuit* in half; it will merely disintegrate. The *mode d'emploi* of this delightful snack begins with butter which must be at or above room temperature for any kind of result. Spread the butter on the *beschuit*, trying not to break the brittle thing. The butter acts as glue for the *muisjes* which are sprinkled on top.

The next step, and biggest challenge, is to eat this delicacy without making too much mess. This takes quite some skill for the inexperienced. Depending on the angle of entry into your mouth, the mice can roll into your lap and onto the floor if the ratio of mice to glue is not correct. Wherever they land, the piles resemble clumps of mouse *shit*. With or without mice, avoid eating a *beschuit* in bed: the crumbs you drop are worse than gritty sand between the sheets.

Beschuit met muisjes is traditionally served on the day the baby is born/comes home from the hospital, so do not be surprised if your grocer wishes you congratulations when you purchase the biscuits and anise sprinkles. Please note that *muisjes* do not also come in blue-and-white as one might suppose. Instead, baby's gender is indicated by the texture of the *muisjes* (rough for boys, smooth for girls). And don't ever confuse *muisjes* with *meisjes!*

Dropjes

The name of the Dutch national nibble is licorice, better known as *drop* or *dropjes*. It comes in all sizes, shapes and flavours, and since they are predominantly black, this helps in differentiating the various cultures. They are sold

pre-packaged or "fresh," the latter being a popular purchase at the local street market. Overdosing on *dropjes* is
known to cause high blood pressure.

In 1990, *cloggies* spent more than HFl 248 million on
dropjes. They are consumed at the rate of 75,000 kg
(165,000 lb) per day. Needless to say, the Dutch *drop*
market is stable and healthy. (One producer uses 25 different recipes.) Among the selection to choose from are:

- soft, chewy fish
- harder-to-chew half moon
- filled baguette
- double-salt parallelogram
- single-salt button
- sweet 'n salty farmhouse
- bite-sized Twizzler
- Belgian boy pissing
- heart-shaped honey drop

- coin-shaped standard
- English mix
- sugar-coated varieties
- traffic signs
- witch's hat design
- cats (in different poses)
- Flintstones characters
- coloured cubes
- spaghetti shoe laces

Sex shops (see Chapter 18) may stock other shapes.

If as a visitor you decide to sample some *drop*, don't be
embarrassed to spit it out after two or three sucks. Most
people do.

Once you decide you definitely don't like the stuff, steer
well clear of a favourite fairground fascination whereby
contestants scoop up ladles of *drop* which they estimate to
be a certain weight – usually 1/2 "Dutch pound" *(pond)*. If
the scooped droppings are exactly the target weight, the
lucky contestants are awarded the batch free of charge. If
the target weight is missed (even by a few milligrams), the
contestants pay for the goodies.

Coveted Cookies . . .

When you are (finally) invited to a Dutch home for a cup of coffee, you will almost certainly be offered a *koekje* (biscuit, cookie) to go with your coffee (see Chapter 14 for coffee drinking etiquette). *Koekje*-offering is a memorable event for foreigners. Typically, once the coffee has been served, a metal box is taken out of an impressive wooden cupboard. The mysterious metal box is opened and you are invited to take a *koekje* -- ONE SINGLE *koekje* -- after which the box is slammed shut and put away again. If you decline the coffee, the *koekje* tin will be offered to all those who have accepted the *koffie*, and you will be by-passed.

Visits to a Dutch home have a regular pattern. First you are invited only for *koffie* and a *koekje*. If you are liked, you may eventually be invited to stay longer than coffee and be served alcoholic drinks and snacks. You've really arrived if you are invited for dinner. Dinners are a special and intimate event for the Dutch. A dinner invitation is not easily given, especially by the older generation.

. . . and Dirty Dishes

If you do stay for dinner, you might be fortunate enough to observe Dutch dish washing (if you don't find yourself doing it) since the dining area often affords a view of this activity. Here is the basic procedure:

- Force a plastic bowl the size of the sink into the sink. Add environment-friendly washing-up liquid, scalding hot water and a sponge (optional).
- Exchanging your sponge for a dish brush (*afwasborsteltje*) with handle, fish an item out of the brutally hot water with the stick-end of the brush.

- Scrub the item clean with the brush-end of the brush. If the item is very deep, ignore the fact that the brush doesn't reach the bottom.
- Once the item is clean, place it in the dish rack, making certain you do not rinse off the soap.
- Let the dish brush sink to the bottom of the basin.
- Make several attempts to fish the brush out of the hot water, and once you succeed, juggle the brush back and forth from left hand to right hand until it cools down enough to use it.
- Search for another item to wash and repeat the process until the bowl appears to be empty. There will always be one or two teaspoons left at the bottom after the procedure is complete.
- If necessary, restock the bowl with dirty dishes and repeat the sequence. If the water is dirty but hot, reuse it. If it is clean but only warm, replace it.
- When all is done, use a towel to rub the soap deposit and any remaining food into the "clean" items.
- Finally – and you're on your own with this one – concoct a method to lift the full, hot, pliant and snugly-fitting bowl from the sink WITHOUT SPILLING THE WATER EVERYWHERE.

Bottom of the Bottle

Cloggy kitchens are also a treasure chest of gadgetry. Best known, perhaps, are the uncleanable garlic press and the slotted spade-like cheese-slicer *(kaasschaaf)* that miraculously produces the stingy, stealth-like slithers of processed curd previously reported. (Try it on anything other than *cloggy **kaas*** and you risk being left with a pile of crumbled crud that resembles a scale model of the walls of Jericho after The Event.)

But by far the most Dutch of Dutch kitchen drawer-ware is the *flessenlikker* or bottle-scraper. This wonderous, flexible wand is a pleasure to both behold and be held. With a few skillful flicks of the wrist, the experienced *flessenlikker* driver can extract enough of those last few elusive smudgettes from a mayonnaise jar or ketchup bottle to (sometimes) save as much as a few cents over a 12-month period. And those last few salvaged remnants taste so much better than the rest of the stuff!

This Dutch-declared device (invented by a Norwegian) has typically met with success only in Holland. It makes an excellent (read: cheap) gift or party piece abroad, as baffled foreigners try to figure out what it is:

- backscratcher?
- part of a lightweight Bicycle pump?
- mini roulette scoop?
- flower-arrangement embellishment?
- feminine hygiene/gay-play device?
- instrument for removing Dutch doggy doo-doo from sufferer's shoe soles?

They'll never guess . . . and probably never want one!

*Wealthy Dutchmen would rather talk about
their sex lives than their money, and their sex
lives are far less interesting.*
J. van Hezewijk, **The Top Elite
of the Netherlands**, 1987

chapter 18

SEX 'N DRUGS
AND
ROCK 'N ROLL

Every society, no matter how wealthy or puritanical, has
its dark side. Having covered the finer elements of the
Dutch in the 17 chapters preceding this, we now turn to the
more infamous aspects. The three major cities of Holland
(Amsterdam, Rotterdam and The Hague) are cities for the
young-at-heart, and the nucleus of open vice, crime and
corruption. In the 1980's, Amsterdam was proclaimed the
CULTURAL capital of Europe; earlier, it acquired, and still
retains, the status of GAY capital of Europe and DRUG capital
of Europe.

In some rural areas, diluted forms of vice, crime and corruption are prevalent. In others, strict Calvinism and other moral standards have stemmed the tide of indecency to the extent that cigarette vending machines are emptied at midnight on Saturdays to prevent trading on a Sunday.

Sex as an Activity

It has been said that the Dutch approach the subject of sex with the warmth and passion of an ice cube. Sex is an act society encourages of individuals aged 14 and up. (In 1987, much pressure was applied to the Government to lower the age of consent from 16 to 12 years.) Many mothers monitor their young teenage daughters for signs of their first menstruation. This is the time to whisk the poor, confused girl to her doctor for her first birth control kit. The male situation is quite different. At the first signs of pubescence, it is not unusual for a Dutch lad to be hounded by his father to experiment with sex, sometimes with no concern for the consequences.

These magnificent displays of understanding and tenderness sow the seeds of sex attitude in the developing children. By the time they reach adulthood, performing the sex act regularly is considered part of the daily routine. In the words of a housewife,

Ja, having sex is something you do in the morning and at night, like brushing your teeth.

Sex can be mentioned coldly but candidly with dinner guests: *"The children had fun at the beach yesterday. We had good sex last night. I must go to the dentist soon."*

Spontaneous stripping and nakedness on the part of *cloggies* should not necessarily be interpreted as a sexual

Part of the daily routine

gesture. They peel off at the slightest excuse and in front of whomever happens to be within visual range. An unwitting visitor meeting a relative for the first time, upon presenting an item of clothing as a gift, may be shocked when the new acquaintance eagerly undresses in front of everyone present in order to try on the clothing. Likewise, visitors to the country are expected to nonchalantly flash their flesh where the natives would. When visiting a doctor, there are no dressing gowns, and patients are expected to undress and remain stark naked in front of the doctor, staff and medical students for the duration of many procedures.

The subject of abortion (a **Vrouwen** birthright) is treated with similar nonchalance:

"Did your period start yet?"
"No, I had an abortion. On the way home, my Bicycle had a puncture . . ."

In an attempt to make sex somewhat interesting, such tantalizing products as illuminating condoms, flavoured condoms and edible underwear are available.

Sex as an Industry

Prostitution grew and flourished in the major cities from the lusting natures of seafarers arriving from long journeys. The Dutch, ever alert to the prospect of easy florins, soon established "red light districts" and even neighbourhoods for the plying of the prostitution trade. These areas are nowadays principally found in the **Randstad**, especially in Amsterdam. With the advent of sexual openness in the western world in the 1960's, these areas have lost their sleaziness and become major tourist attractions. Prostitutes accept major credit cards, cheques, foreign currency -- anything that represents MONEY. They exude pride in their profession (making no attempt to disguise their business); attend regular medical check-ups which are organized by the local Government; and enjoy a healthy relationship with the tax officials who will generally grant deductions for a range of occupational necessities.

Due to the social advantages of fucking for funds in Holland, a large foreign element exists among the prostitute community (in The Hague, more than 25% of prostitutes hold non-Dutch passports). They enter the country, work for three months and claim a tax refund prior to leaving *"as a traveling circus through Europe."* All is not plain sailing, however, as many complain about the difficulties of getting Moroccan, Turkish and even many Dutch men to *"hoist a condom."*

The **Rode Draad** (Red Thread) organisation, representing *cloggy* ladies of pleasure (and, presumably, gentlemen of pleasure), frequently protests governmental attempts to tighten up on things such as lighting, toilets, wash facilities and working arrangements. As with all Dutch organisations, they have their own set of membership demands. Among these demands are:

- Permit prostitutes *(sexwerkers)* to choose whether they work in a club or independently. *"Prostitution is a creative profession that requires creative rules."*
- Exempt prostitutes from revealing their true names for official purposes.
- Provide improved conditions and benefits such as social security, sick pay, special tax tariffs, pension benefits, pregnancy leave and compensation for time off during menstruation.

Perhaps the best compromise for this conflict would be to instigate partial Government ownership of the industry, wherein the sex business owners would receive subsidies from local Government departments (health, occupational hazards, tourism and art) to improve the quality of service for all to enjoy: the Dutch Civil Cervix.

Nowhere in this particular conflict does the subject of suppressing open prostitution occur. The main opposition to open prostitution comes from the regiment of liberated **Vrouwen** (see Chapter 11) who view the emancipated, enterprising "ladies of pleasure" as a disease infecting the decent and honest Dutch way of life . . .

. . . Thus, those who campaign for women's freedom and independence are the ones that object most severely to women having achieved that status.

In the early 1990's, a HFl 300,000 experiment to establish a *"tolerance zone"* for prostitution in the city of
Arnhem failed. The tolerance zone collapsed due to action
and protest by local residents who posted some 20 people
in the area from 9 pm to 2 am every evening for four
months. This created an atmosphere which the press reported was *"too threatening and not anonymous enough for
prostitutes and relief workers to start the programme."* This
gave rise to yet another experiment whereby free heroin
would be given to addicted street prostitutes . . .

Eventually, the national Government relented and made
prostitution legally legal -- and therefore legally taxable.
*"We want to get this business out of the criminal sphere and
subject it to strict regulations regarding health standards, labour conditions and public order,"* explained legislator
Marian Soutendijk. The love-ladies had a different interpre-
tation: *"We're effectively getting another pimp,"* blasted a
spokes*vrouw* for the national prostitutes' union.

To further stress the point that penis payment is pro-
foundly permissible, a high court ruled that a severely
handicapped man was entitled to a HFl 65- monthly grant
towards the cost of a female "sex aid worker." The sum
involved was ruled no great burden on the local Government (Noordoostpolder). The man's claim to entitlement
was based on a psychological report which concluded that
he had need of sex once a month. Form a line here please,
gentlemen!

For those who prefer synthetic sex, the availability of all
things pornographic is overwhelming. Sex shops are in
such abundance that one can rarely pass through more
than two streets in larger city interiors without spotting a
shop window openly displaying devices, films, clothing and
literature of a diverse sexual nature. Competition is so

sharp that specialist sex shops (gay, lesbian, child, etc.) are also open for business.

Drugs I – Still Smokin'

The heavily reported Dutch over-tolerant attitude towards drug abuse is almost as famous as their tulips and wooden shoes, but it should be noted that the most active areas are in the *Randstad*, with relatively little activity in villages and the countryside. Progressive Dutch attitude excludes soft drugs such as cannabis/hashish and marijuana from the "problem drugs" category.

What seems shocking to tourists is run-of-the-(wind)mill for the urban Dutch. In Amsterdam, it is normal to see marijuana plants growing in homes and occasionally even in public places. The locals think nothing of smoking a "joint" in public. The Cannabis Café, or Hash Café *(hasj-café)* abounds, gloriously announced by a marijuana leaf painted on the front window and/or outside sign. Ironically, many of these specialist shops are not licensed to sell beverages of an intoxicating nature. From the Dutch medical point of view, soft drugs are considered harmless when compared with the more socially-accepted alcoholic indulgence.

The existence of soft drug establishments, which were first introduced in 1975, relies on the national obsession with social tolerance being a greater force than the law. The 1976 Opium Act prohibits the importing, trafficking and possession of "soft," succulent smoking substances. However, possession and selling of less than 30 grams are classed as mere misdemeanours (along with riding a Bike without lights at night, or pissing in public places). The Dutch Government's stamp of non-disapproval comes with carefully crafted comments: *"We see no harm in possessing*

A Cannabis Café

or using soft drugs . . .," announced a Ministry of Justice spokes*vrouw, ". . . (users) stop after a certain age. We hope people who want to try soft drugs don't go to people who sell hard drugs."*

The question arises as to how the Hash Cafés restock their supplies, since no traffic jams caused by wholesalers delivering their goods in 30g increments are ever reported. *"I don't know,"* confessed an Amsterdam police spokesman. *"I can't tell you that,"* revealed the proprietor of one such establishment.

The current generation of *cloggies* are mavens in soft drugs. Hash Cafés stock various varieties of seeds and young plants, soil enrichers and pots. For the more serious smoker, proprietors are only too willing to guide customers in their purchases by process of elimination based on the anticipated growing-environment:

- indoors, outdoors, greenhouse
- harvesting time
- direction of prevailing natural light
- soil.

The local authorities keep their lenient eyes on the industry, estimated at HFl 650 million per year. If a marijuana merchant exceeds the tolerance zone, the enterprise is closed down. Although ventures such as pre-cooked "Space Cakes" and the "Blow Home Courier Service" have been forced to close, others such as the Hash Taxi (see Chapter 3) are encouraged to continue.

Drugs II – The Hard Line

Hard drugs are less openly traded. The merchants comprise an army of solicitors of various minority groups who hustle for customers at main railway stations, monuments, public parks, youth centres, red light districts, etc. In theory, possession of hard drugs is illegal. In practice, users are not arrested; only the (bulk) dealers are liable for prosecution.

For some years, an "innovative approach" was to give the dealers and junkies their own part of town -- the Zeedijk in Amsterdam -- where they were allowed to do business. The idea was to be kind and open to dealers and junkies while concentrating their activities to a specific area. The result? In the words of Eduard van Thijn, then Mayor of Amsterdam, *"We thought we could be tolerant and still control hard drugs. We were very naive."*

One of the constructive aspects of the Dutch view on the unfortunate reality of hard drug addiction is that the authorities adopt the attitude that *"These people are ill and should be helped, not persecuted."* In support of this doctrine, methadone buses freely distribute this substance in major cities to help addicts withdraw from their dependence on heroin. The buses stop at known points in the city for about an hour and a half to dispense the drug free of charge.

Crime and Punishment

Convictions for drug trafficking (and other criminal activities) are sometimes never served. With prisons stocked to capacity and due to the Dutch tendency towards forgiveness, sentences are often extremely lenient. Prison terms are served on a space availability basis. Thus, a criminal (sorry, "victim of society") will be released upon conviction, pending an empty cell. If a criminal does go to jail, chances are his or her stay will be carried out in relative comfort. The idea is to provide the prisoners with as normal a lifestyle as possible. At Schutterswei, a jail in Alkmaar, prisoners are paid around HFl 55- a week. Many use the money to decorate and furnish their private "cells" with televisions, stereos, pets and, of course, a *koffie*-maker. A special private visitor's room -- "sex cell" -- is provided, complete with furniture (including a bed), paintings and carpet. Other privileges, or in this case RIGHTS, include wearing one's own clothing, access to a kitchen to cook one's own meals if so desired, the right to vote, freedom to speak to journalists and a system for expressing and debating complaints.

It is part design and part necessity that the Dutch have instigated forms of "alternative punishment" and "educational projects" in order to rehabilitate their victims of society. Such forms of punishment may include a 22-day excursion to a mountain camp on the Mediterranean coast, enjoying the local countryside and cuisine.

Consequently, theft from automobiles is commonplace, as is pickpocketing and similar crimes. To have your car broken into and the HFl 500- radio-cassette player stolen is considered no big event.

The attitude of the police? One of inconvenience – your ex-property will be on sale in a bar the next evening where you can buy it back for HFl 60-, and you must be grateful for such a bargain!

Rock 'n Roll, etc. . . .

It must be said that the Dutch are, as a nation, appreciative of music – contemporary and otherwise. Cities and towns provide a wealth of music venues to suit all tastes and (sub)cultures. Even small villages sport at least one location where varied, live music can be heard.

Music lovers? Yes. Innovators? No. *Cloggies* love to copy. Be it classical, traditional, modern or free-form jazz, they will copy recognized, accomplished performers to the last semi-quaver. In Amsterdam alone, one can walk along the inner-city shopping precincts on a Saturday and revel in a multiplicity of street- and *café*-musicians including at least:

- one **Dutch** highland bagpiper, complete with full Scots regalia of bearskin, tunic and kilt/sporran
- one **Dutch** traditional Irish session group, equipped with fiddles, mandolins, bodhran drums, bones and pints of Guinness

- one **Dutch** Mozart string quartet, optionally dressed in jeans or tails, and displaying music stands containing faded, manuscript sheet music
- dozens of contemporary-bard stereotypes of the 1960's Dylan/Donovan variety, equipped with aging acoustic guitar and tattered guitar case (covered in stickers) at their feet for "contributions."

A wandering minstrel

Yet Holland is a country for the young at heart. And the food of youth is Rock 'n Roll. In Amsterdam, Rock venues abound, openly selling mainly-imported Hard Rock music, alcohol and drugs to the age group 14+. Inaptly described as "multi-media centres" or "youth clubs," the more infamous include the Paradiso and the Melkweg in the equally infamous Leidseplein area. Rotterdam and The Hague have their equivalents.

On a less lavish scale, but by no means small in number are the Rock Cafés -- bars steaming with "heavy metal" fans who drink, smoke and dope their way to oblivion between the hours of 8 pm and 2 am.

The drink is the locally-brewed Heineken or Amstel Pilsener beer. The smoke-and-dope is mainly cigarettes (*Camel* brand for the males and liberated females; *Pall Mall* for the females and liberated males), marijuana and hashish -- all washed down with lashings of hot Rock music, provided via the medium of modern, high-quality Japanese electronics.

I only miss Holland when I'm in Holland.
Paul Verhoeven,
Hollywood Film Director, 1992

chapter 19

THE FLYING DUTCHMAN

export models

D utch persons migrate. They have to. If they didn't, they wouldn't all fit in Holland. When they migrate, they take their *clogginess* with them and shed it kilo-by-kilo as their newly-adopted culture requires, with a pinch of protest thrown in for good measure. Some traits persist; some are relinquished willingly, others begrudgingly.

They migrate through an osmosis-like process whereby they assimilate into their new-found culture so easily and so well that even they at times appear to forget their roots.

But they rarely lose their heritage and revert to type whenever convenient or satisfying for the ego.

The World According to Jaap

To the uninitiated, the reasons *cloggies* emigrate may appear rather illusive. Dutch immigrants like to make reference to profundities such as: *"for certain reasons," "for my own choice," "because of various things that are important to me,"* but will rarely tell you WHY. It soon becomes apparent that the main factor for leaving Heaven is MORE: more money, more living space, more freedom from domineering relatives, more opportunities. In terms of emigration for economics, the Dutch are no different than anyone else. When it comes to crowds and nosy, interfering relatives, they have more to escape from than most. Immigration allows them to shed those properties that they felt compelled to conform to as a part of their devout Dutchness.

They take refuge in such places as Australia, Canada, New Zealand, South Africa, the USA and their ex-colonies. The wooden shoes, windmills, dikes, and so forth, are packaged and go with them. These symbols are subsequently summoned to perform services, as required. Once successfully migrated, the post-Holland Hollander will immediately pronounce *"Ja! I am Dutch, but I am not like the others. I would not be here and now if I was!"*

When challenged, many view their homeland as utopia corrupted: *"How Holland has changed since I was there!"* It is as if THEIR parting has turned Someren into Sodom and Groningen into Gommorah.

They love to BE Dutch and to knock it at the same time. They abhor the image of the three W's, tulips and blond-plaited maidens in traditional costume and rigorously reprimand their unwitting hosts who (dare) associate these superficial symbols with Holland. Yet when the same people need some heritage or history, out come the wooden shoes, windmills, tulips and feigned costumes.

The break is not always complete. Friends and relatives flock to the new nest. The prospect of a cheap vacation and visiting a foreign land without the encumbrance of travel inconveniences is irresistible to those left behind. Although such rekindling can be *leuk* (nice) where (grand)children are concerned, it also volunteers to be a pain for the re-liberated emigrants who have to be constantly reminded of WHO and WHAT they are, and from WHENCE they came:

The Dutch people I know come to visit from Holland, uninvited, for 12 weeks or so. During that time, they expect more or less to be catered to, to be driven around and expect you to tour with them whether you have work to do or not. They don't think they have to help with the grocery bill, but they WILL tell you when the beer is gone or there are no more chips.
Only in the last four years have I come to think of this as IMPOSING on people in a major way.

M. Mol, British Columbia

The degree to which the immigrants retain or relinquish specific values varies from land to land. In some cases, local politics and/or economics have eradicated certain of the most beloved behaviours. The influence of the local culture and customs, and freedom from former social and bureaucratic pressures, also play a significant role in this reshaping process. One factor in the equation appears to be the size of the country in question. In this respect, the general rule seems to be:

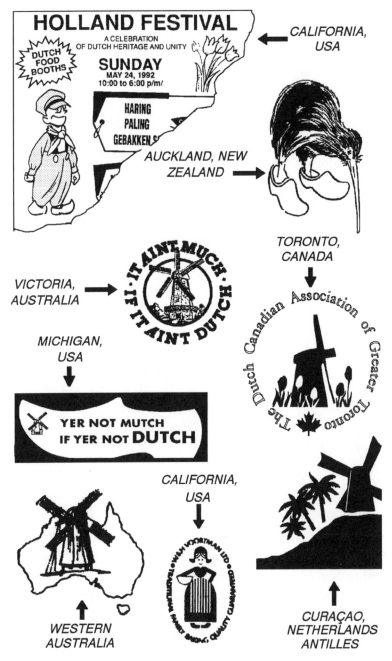

Shedding the image

---

*Retention of national nature
is inversely proportional to the size
of the adopted land mass.*

A common factor is that the immigrants feel no compunction about enlisting the local labour as servants whenever and wherever customary. Far away from their homeland, they feel no guilt or remorse at "exploiting" their fellow human beings in a way that would cause widespread disquiet back home. It appears to be justified by:

- the old adage *When in Rome . . .*
- *We help the economy by providing employment.*
- *We treat them well.*

Of late in some countries, there is a growing trend to reduce the number (or completely eliminate the use) of servants, but only *"because they are becoming more and more expensive. You must OVERPAY for their low productivity."*

The Right Stuff

When abroad, all nationalities are drawn to memories of home, hence the success of English fish-'n-chip shops, American hamburger joints and oriental restaurants.

Understandably, the Dutch cuisine (see Chapter 17) is not so represented, but another lifeline is: Beer. Usually paraded as "HEINEKEN EXPORT -- brewed in Holland" or the Amstel/Grolsch equivalent, renegade Hollanders will flock to the stuff like iron filings to a magnet and orgasmically utter:

"Ahhh! [BRAND NAME] -- so much better than [LOCAL BREW]!"

and then confess:

"But this is entirely different to what is sold in Holland."

On realizing what they have just confessed to, a qualification is added:

"I think it is better. Only a Dutch brewery could do something like this!"

This attitude is strongly endorsed by the breweries themselves. In the words of Alfred Lord Heineken,

We are a Rolls Royce abroad, in Holland just a normal beer.

Oh, the humility of it all!

Uses for Rolls Royce packaging -- monkey cage cover . . .

. . . native dolls' house . . .

. . . the coconut cupboard

Nowhere is the concept of *cloggy* camaraderie more pronounced than in the seemingly endless supply of overseas Dutch clubs, friendship societies, newspapers, newsletters, gourmet shops, Tulip Festivals, Heritage Days and the inevitable Queen's Birthday celebration. The latter events provide an excuse for genuine Dutch immigrants to dust off all the Neder-paraphernalia and related junk that they imported under the guise of "household goods" and display it with gay (old definition) abandon as part of their heritage, tradition, etc.

Dutch fraternity is focused on just about anyone with a "*van*" or "*de*" in their name. The fate of these identity prefixes is interesting in itself. *Van de* and *Van der* either become a single prefix (*Vander Meulen*) or no prefix at all (*Vandergronden, Vandenberg*). The "*ij*" becomes a "*y*" (*Wijnbelt* to *Wynbelt*). The spellings of some names are changed to facilitate pronunciation (*Geert* and *Gert* melt into *Kert*). This process of identity preservation-integration is epitomized in a plea from a newsletter published by the New Zealand-Netherlands Society Oranje Auckland, Inc., which published a request for readers to submit ideas for a society logo. The plea gave the following suggestions:

> *. . . A coat hanger with a pair of clogs hanging from it?*
> *An outline of Rangitoto Island with a windmill on top?*

Flower fascination is not forsaken abroad. Lowland-leavers lavish love upon their favourite bulbs and bushes in every corner of the world. When they leave Holland, they are absolutely delighted to find themselves surrounded by relatively enormous garden plots (and usually more sunshine) in which they can grow an abundance of flowers -- or even better, fields of wildflowers -- thereby saving on florist bills. In an inherently efficient manner, many take their cultivation-cunning with them and frequently engage in entrepreneurial and lucrative greenhouse and nursery ventures. Those who are fortunate enough to own and operate their own retail outlets subtly hint at the source of their super blooms, as demonstrated below.

Flogging flowers in Florida

The Dutch have been highly successful in farming. Not only are their farms very productive, but their flexibility and ability to migrate have also added to their earnings. For example, they have been known to purchase large areas of fertile land, convert them into profitable agricultural regions and later sell the whole thing for a "small" fortune as prime real estate.

Further fundamentals include *koffie*, *gezellig*-ness and thriftiness (to the point of continually coveting *koekjes*). One of the first things to be perused is the quality of the local coffee. If it is undrinkably weak and tasteless (as opposed to customarily weak and tasteless), then *koffie* will be placed on the lifeline supply list. (Other essential items include *dropjes*, *erwtensoep* and *jenever* gin.)

They have anchored their architecture wherever possible throughout history. Their famous gables, draw-bridges and windmills are often found where they have reigned or prospered. Large and luscious *landhuizen* (manor houses, plantation homes) of old are the subject of renovation around the globe. In more recent times, quaint shopping streets with storybook facades as well as wind-mill restaurants and souvenir shops have been built or restored as major tourist attractions.

Perhaps the most important ingredient that kept early immigrants united and determined to succeed against all odds was their religious conviction(s). With the passing of time (and with a few classic exceptions, such as some Dutch Reformed Church/Calvinist elements), most of the devout religious communities have since disappeared.

Complaint and criticism prevail, albeit in a diluted form (gone is the thirst for protests and demonstrations). Dutch immigrants criticize life in their host country, comparing it to their wonderful *Nederland*. Things perceived as being better than in Holland are not generally acknowledged in the new land, but are held in reserve for the next visit home. This is necessary as their absence will have prevented them from keeping abreast of current complain-able topics. Thus the only way to maintain a homecoming conversation is to neutralize the nonsense by bragging about their wise move abroad, the relative cost of things (necessary to prevent alienation), the freedom from governmental regulations and the abundance of space.

Somewhere along the path, some of *The Right Stuff* becomes *The Wrong Stuff*. The main victim appears to be The Bicycle, which is tragically disowned in the most stressful and traumatic parting ever experienced by a *cloggy*. The Bicycle as a protected species, having survived the perilous journey to foreign lands, cannot cohabitate with cultures which do not understand the necessity for the *fietspad*, riders' rights or Bike hospitals/hostels. Ironically, the final blow to the devices is served by the immigrants themselves who put the contraptions to shed because of the reasons they deserted their homeland:

- DISTANCES -- having escaped the cramped conditions in Holland's towns and cities, there is now too much space to contemplate cycling everywhere over heretofore unheard-of distances.
- CLIMATE -- favourite lands to adopt typically enjoy hot summers and/or violent winters. *Cloggy* pedal power soon exhausts itself under these generally uncomfortable conditions.
- TERRAIN -- the addition of a vertical component to the landscape (mountains and valleys) introduces rugged, steep roads and generally unfriendly conditions.

Another casualty is language, unless both parents make a concerted effort to speak Dutch at home. This is rarely the case.

Colonial Cloggies

The Dutch colonized part of the East and West Indies for about three centuries. In general, their behaviour was much the same as that of other colonizing nations – a general plundering of land and people. The attitude, however, was coloured by their Calvinistic heritage:

- On the one hand, they would not allow extreme poverty, hardship or cruel rituals to persist.
- On the other hand, they kept themselves remote and somewhat aloof from the entirely different mentality of the colonized populations.

Indonesia . . .

Great difficulties in the Dutch East Indies were caused by Netherlandic ambivalence towards the old Indonesian rulers who were allowed to continue to reign, but under strict Dutch regulations. The East Indies were a source of great wealth and aided Holland during the economic crisis in the 1930's. World War II and the Japanese occupation contributed to the cultural chaos in the region's post-war period. Holland experienced untold problems in reasserting authority. A premature independence came to Indonesia in the late 1940's, causing a forced mass migration of not only the true Dutch but also some 500,000 Eurasians whose only sin was that of their parents' desires.

Nowadays Dutch involvement in the country is reversed. They are generally short-term residents involved with aid/agricultural projects, etc., and of a generation who feel a certain guilt over their forefathers' activities.

They are in their element as far as creature comforts are concerned. The local coffee and tea are *lekker*, cheap and abundant. Many of the older houses are typically old-Dutch style, and the popularity of the local food (at far less than Dutch prices) goes without saying. Typically, the Indonesian language is mastered in no time, even for the lesser-educated Hollanders whose pre-arrival skills tend to be limited to the vital *bami goreng, loempia* and *saté*.

Many of the Netherlanders are perceived by others as *"the typically loony/aging hippy types and not the highly sophisticated types."* Whatever type they may be, they throw themselves into the community and seem to love every minute of it. This Indonesian immersion applies to those who elect to remain on a permanent basis to such an extent that they almost stop being Dutch. However, offspring are commonly cursed with pressures to develop the forceful personality of the true *cloggy*.

The biggest threat to this utopia of theirs is The Hague's refusal to stop interfering in its ex-colony's affairs. In 1992, the Dutch Government overtly criticized atrocities by the Indonesian army. This angered President Suharto who then announced that his country would like to be rid of the HFl 350 million of annual aid.

Netherlands Antilles & Aruba . . .

The Kingdom of the Netherlands consists of three parts: Holland, Aruba and the 4-1/2 islands of the Netherlands Antilles (Curaçao, Bonaire, Saba, St. Eustatius and 0.5 x St. Maarten). Hollanders grabbed the Antilles in the 17th century. They had found their tropical paradise:

- lack of size (islands range from 5-180 sq. miles)
- abundance of water
- lack of elevation (only one proper hill, plus one volcanic rock).
  IT WAS PERFECT.

In true European style, they then spent the next century or so spoiling it. At first came the "gingerbread houses," slave huts, drawbridges, canals, ports and prostitution. Later, the need for lego-roads (and yellow DAF-like buses to destroy them), banks, road roundabouts with traffic lights, *Sinterklaas & Zwarte Piet, Koninginnedag*, lotto and topless sunbathing beaches was satisfied. The official language is Dutch, the local currency is the (Netherlands Antilles) guilder, and hotel/restaurant food is bland and boring. The result is a tropical home-from-home which can act as a tax haven for the rich and an exotic Caribbean Holland-like getaway for the rest. All of this, of course, has been achieved by reprogramming the native population.

The Antilles strongly depend upon Netherlandness for their survival and prosperity. The practice of Hollanders to use Antillean services for acquiring driving licences (see Chapter 13) is but one example. Basically, the motherland is only involved with finances from an aloof distance.

The tourist industry preys heavily on the *cloggy* connection. Thus, top priority is given to renovating, decorating and constructing traditional quaint structures. All the basic souvenirs -- delftware, wooden shoes and lewd T-shirts -- are on sale, in addition to the local island goodies. Resident Dutch merchants readily admit that they prefer American tourists to their own kind since, *"A tourist tends to buy the same overall amount of souvenirs during a visit, whether spending one week or one month on the islands."* And with their generous holiday allowance, the Hollanders spend a minimum of three weeks on the island(s) and tend not to buy souvenirs imported from Holland, whereas Americans do so in excess.

To the Dutch residents, island life is at times reminiscent of village life back home. On the glamorous side, life can be cosy and secure with a fixed daily routine, favourite hang-outs, familiar faces, **koffie uurtjes**, visits to the local baker, etc. But with the mentality of a small village come the usual problems of nosy neighbours, false friendliness, excessive envy and gossip. Add the element of foreign territory and you get the usual boasting *("my pool," "my housemaid," "my suntan")* and complaining *("too hot," "too many insects," "too primitive")*. The compulsory clique who miss everything about Holland take no comfort in the fact that the local supermarket imports most traditional tasty treats.

Antilles architecture (look familiar?)

The never-say-no mind-set of the natives is a truly trying experience with which the straightforward Hollander has to come to terms. Antilleans and Arubans consider it polite and proper to say "yes" (and thus make impossible promises) and rude to say "no." Merge this with the regional *mañana* mentality of being late by several hours, days or weeks for appointments or whatever, and it is enough to make any self-respecting Netherlander high-tail it home to show off his tan in the civilized world of chapters 2 through 18.

Suriname . . .

Originally sighted by one of Columbus' crew, Suriname came under Dutch control in 1667. It officially became a Dutch colony the same year when the English gave up their claims to it as a consolation prize for the Dutch loss of the state of New York, then New Amsterdam (see "New World Netherlanders," this chapter).

Suriname was, and is, Holland's answer to North America's Deep South -- a territory where white entrepreneurs used African slave labour to cultivate specialized crops (one of the most important here being coffee). The set-up was Calvinistically correct, provided slaves were not sold to Iberian customers. (Such a trade would have exposed the merchandise to *"the abuses and perils of popery."*)

For years the Netherlanders secretly cultivated coffee in Suriname. They took great care to prevent Brazil (known in part as "New Holland" until the Dutch were expelled) from acquiring any beans. The whole enterprise foundered when a Brazilian espionage mission managed to smuggle THE BEAN out of the country. This broke the Dutch monopoly and gave rise to the Brazilian coffee empire. The Surinamese economy crumbled further when slavery was abolished.

Suriname remained a Dutch colony until 1954 when it became a self-governing state within the Kingdom of the Netherlands. In 1975, it became the independent Republic of Suriname. At this time, large numbers of Surinamese immigrated to the Netherlands, causing a shortage of skilled labour. This is cited as a reason to frequently ask for financial help from Holland.

Cruelties on the side of an absolute military regime in the early 1980's led the Dutch to stop financial aid, and the country economically went to shambles (again). The political situation has improved somewhat, but the Netherlands Government still has doubts about granting financial aid to a third-world country whose natives basically behave the way they were taught. The Surinamese understandably use the word *patata* (potato) to refer to their ex-masters.

The native population is around 350,000 while there are around 200,000 Surinamese in Holland. Tourism in Suriname is almost non-existent. It comes as no surprise that the country is not a favourite location for contemporary *cloggies*, except for those with family or business ties -- and the adventurous types. The situation is basically a disaster as far as the modern-day Dutchman is concerned.

The Pretorian Disgard

Contrary to popular belief, South Africa was never a Dutch colony or territory. Holland first infiltrated the region in 1652 to establish supply routes and rest stations. In order to break away from English colonizers, the Dutch explored the unsettled northeast where they founded the independent republics of Transvaal and the Orange Free State. They considered themselves *Afrikaners*. The final severance of bloodline bonds came when Holland declined to support them in the Boer wars.

The Afrikaans language developed from 17th-century Dutch. The first Dutch settlers spoke country dialects and often wrote phonetically. Many *cloggies* consider Afrikaans to be a form of pidgin Dutch or a mere dialect. In 1925, Afrikaans replaced Dutch as one of the country's two official languages -- English being the second -- and remains the native language of much of South Africa to this day.

As time and politics progressed, the region came to define two distinct breeds of Dutch extract:

- *AFRIKANERS:* Born in the country; despite their Dutch descent, strongly consider themselves "white" Africans, with no feeling of being Dutch.
- *HOLLANDERS:* Immigrants; will never be considered *Afrikaners.* They are nicknamed *kaaskop/ kaaskoppe* (blockhead -- lit.,"cheese head") and *Japie/Jaap* (simpleton/lout).

Holland's interest in South Africa has had many peaks and troughs. Discovery of gold and diamonds (1870's) was an obvious peak, and the introduction and continued practice of apartheid (1948-1992) was definitely a trough. Sadly, the attitude of apartheid still festers the minds of some *Afrikaners* and *Hollanders* who charge Holland with much of the cause of its demise (see panel, opposite).

Hollanders fear that their lifestyle will soon be changed forever. They defend it for its positive points and the hope of a brighter future for all. They reject completely the image of Boer-born Dutchmen portrayed by author Tom Sharpe in *Riotous Assembly* and *Indecent Exposure,* where Luitenant Verkramp, Konstabel Els and Co. are seen as brutal, racist law enforcers, giving the natives only what they deserve.

In general, it is thought that Holland has overreacted to the situation here due to lack of sufficient knowledge of the local circumstances and that the emotional approach is to a large extent inspired by domestic (Dutch) political considerations. TV news coverage and other forms of the media exaggerate things.
H.H.H. (Port Elizabeth)

The Dutch get along fairly well with the blacks, but the blacks have an entirely different mentality. This is something that is not realized overseas. The blacks come out of a tribal existence. When the world says, "You must have democracy in South Africa," the blacks don't understand what democracy is. They are used to one leader or chief who tells them what to do. When they get the power, as in other African countries, they become very autocratic and corrupt, and just a few people prosper while the rest suffer and/or starve. Blacks work much slower, steal, break and damage. So how can you give them equal pay? If you pay them too much, they won't come back until the money is gone!
H.A. (Pretoria)

There is mutual respect between all the races here. The blacks are much better off in South Africa than in the rest of Africa. To hell with the Dutch. They don't know what's going on in South Africa. They sit in their ivory towers and judge us from afar.
N.S. (Expatriate Afrikaner)

Holland has gone downhill morally.
H.M.J. de J.(Johannesburg)

For some, the only way out is to get out. But again the reasoning varies. One readily admits . . .

The way things are now, we are considering leaving Zuid Afrika. Once the black Government takes over here, we don't want to be here!

. . . while another prepares for a new, new life in the Netherlands with an overhauled attitude:

I would cry if the wooden clog was the symbol of Holland!

The feeling back home is understandably strong and offers a refreshing counterpoint to the views expressed on the preceding page:

The comments are a clear example of the difficulties the world has to face before a definite goal will be reached. Fortunately, a lot of people in South Africa (and not only the "blacks") have a much more well-balanced and differentiated view towards these problems than the opinions printed on these pages.
                    Dr. W. Stortenbeek (Apeldoorn, Holland)

We can only agree with and support Dr. Stortenbeek's assessment (and Dutch sentiment in general) on this touchy subject.

Down-Under Dutch

It is difficult to imagine water-denying dikes constructed in the parched outback of Australia, or tulip fields invading the rich sheep-grazing areas of New Zealand, but the purveyors are there.

In general, they are a well-respected, hard-working bunch.

Australia . . .

Hard-working and hard-playing -- exactly the image that Australia likes to portray. Here we have perhaps the most successful Dutch integration of all the lands discussed in this chapter.

The *cloggy* invasion peaked in the 1950's and early 1960's with the support of Dutch religious and governmental organizations. There are 24 Dutch language radio programmes around Australia, and weekly and monthly newspapers, plus many social, community and religious clubs. Dutch press scoops include world-shattering news items such as "TASMANIAN COWS GIVE MORE MILK THAN THEIR INTERSTATE COUSINS," and "PHILIPS LIGHT BULBS ILLUMINATE THE SYDNEY HARBOUR BRIDGE."

To the Dutch-Australian, the most beloved person to have ever set foot on Australian soil was the little-known navigator:

ABEL JANSZOON TASMAN

Apparently, Grootegast-born Abel discovered the lump of land at the bottom right of Australia in 1642 on orders from then Governor of Java, Anthony Van Diemen. Abel named the place after Anthony, Anthony said *bedankt*, and Australia renamed it Tasmania ("Tassie" or "Tas" for short). And so that is what it has since become to the Hollanders that live there: Tas-MANIA.

To celebrate the Tasman Trip's 350th anniversary, Dutch-Australians conspired to give Abel his well-deserved recognition (although he sailed around Australia without even seeing it) by organizing, amongst other things:

- a year-long Abel Tasman Festival (in Hobart)
- the Dutch-Australian Society "Abel Tasman," Inc.
- the Abel Tasman Commemorative Medallion
- unveiling of an Abel Tasman coastal monument
- the Circumnavigation of Tasmania yacht crews
- the Abel Tasman Blue Water Classic Yacht Race
- the Abel Tasman Yachting Cup
- guided heritage (?) tours to the Abel Tasman landing site
- Dutch civic visits including the Mayor of Grootegast and the Governor of Groningen.

Tasman gave the Australian continent its first European name: New Holland (original, huh?). As if this isn't enough, more of the Abel Aftermath of discovering the southern hemisphere Holland includes:

- tulip festivals that attract thousands of visitors
- *oliebollen* festivals that attract thousands of visitors
- infestation of Dutch-sounding or -looking place names, such as Zeehan, Geeveston, Schouten and Maatsuyker
- world record for Tasman-named names (e.g. Tasman Sea, Tasman Basin, South Tasmanian Rise, Tasman Hills, Tasmanian wolf (or tiger), Tasmanian devil).

Australia has a permanent effect on the Dutch who have lived there. One settler who returned to the Netherlands has this to say about her rediscovered homeland:

When I returned to Holland from Australia, I found it was difficult to adjust to the lack of nature and space, and also lack of clean bodies of water.
The Netherlands is regulated to the extent that it breeds resistance. Opening hours for shops are very restricted. Swimming pools open to "outsiders" (non-ethnic, male, singles, etc.) during certain hours only. There are waiting lists for many things, especially accommodation. If you don't fit in an "urgent" category, you have to wait years.
There is racism and people of colour are not treated as citizens. It is hard to make friends. It entails responsibilities, involves keeping in regular touch, a keen interest on both sides. Thus one can spend many hours on weekends traveling to and from friends to satisfy the moral obligation.

This attitude from a repatriated Hollander seems hard to understand, until one considers that perhaps the reason for the venomous voice is because she no longer QUALIFIES for preferential treatment. Maybe Dutchness ain't so dead in Australia after all!

One thing that will never die is the stubborn adherence to one of the strongest hereditary weaknesses known to *clog*dom: the rivalry between their best-loved brews -- Heineken and Amstel beers. But here the two have learned the art of **samen wonen** and live peaceably in sin in beach-front bliss in areas where their patrons are plentiful and well out of sight of their *Fosters* parents.

A Dutch "kroeg" -- Australian style

New Zealand . . .

Originally named Nieuw Zeeland by its discoverer who never landed there (you guessed it -- Abel Tasman), the country was renamed New Zealand by its British owners (who kept the "Z" to keep the *cloggies* happy). Before we discuss the New Zealand Netherlanders, let's get the Abel-worship out of the way. The year 1992 marked the 350th anniversary of "the sighting" and was of course designated Abel Tasman Year, as defined and reflected by the:

- New Zealand Abel Tasman 1992 Commission.
- Auckland 1992 Abel Tasman Memorial Fund
- Abel Tasman Commemorative Stamp

- Annual Tulip Queen & Abel Tasman Competition
- Abel Tasman tulip field dedication
- Cartography exhibition
- Dutch food and Fashion Festival
- Books, TV documentaries, sports events, etc.
- Closing Abel Tasman Year Function.

(Here endeth the lesson on caning Abel.)

Cloggies complain that New Zealanders are too English:

The New Zealanders are more English than the English. They haven't got their own identity yet. This irritates us. They are too reserved and are not open. In Holland, we got to know our neighbours, but not in New Zealand. The people are too polite to tell you what they really think.

In New Zealand more than in any other country the Dutch regret giving up their passion to protest for pleasure and possession:

I really accuse [my fellow] Dutch people of being too quiet and too polite here. We should have made waves because other groups did and got something for it.

Although NZ-NL'ers boast, *"We are well known for our great integration skills in this country,"* they afford perhaps the greatest living example of the perseverance of "The Dutch Way" overseas. There are only 70,000 of 'em (3% of the total population), but NZ-NL'ers will not compromise their position or attitude for any reason:

- In 1967, two opposing factions of the Dutch community started to war over the rights to a publication title. A mere word or two relating to *Clogdom* is apparently so important that by

1973, the issue had reached the Privy Council in London, England (the gloriously highest court in Her Britannic Majesty's Commonwealth of Great Britain and Northern Ireland). Despite a definitive ruling, the parties are still at odds over the issue. The wording in question? "THE WINDMILL POST."

- A community radio broadcaster in Auckland is operated by a group of young Dutch immigrants. The station has refused to acknowledge this book as the origin of the name of their nightly programme, pleading, *"Our programme is called 'RADIO Undutchables' not 'THE UnDutchables' so there's no total usage of your book title. We receive no renumeration whatsoever so there is no commercial gain,"* rather than submit to common decency and give a 10-second acknowledgement on the air. So much for the importance of originality in Netherlandic titles when an outsider is involved.

- The victor in the Windmill Post feud has launched a follow-on campaign. The latest target is the New Zealand Government, which is charged with, for example, illegally taxing pensions paid by the Netherlands to retired Dutch emigrants. This one looks as if it could reach the international court in The Hague for a final ruling.

Many immigrant NZ-NL'ers are disillusioned by what they feel is job discrimination against the Dutch:

In New Zealand, hiring is by nationality and not by qualifications. The best jobs go to native English speakers: the English, then the Americans, then the New Zealanders. It is hard for the rest to get good jobs here. We are considered foreigners.

VOL. 42   NR. 4   **AUGUST 1992**

Windmill Post

NEW ZEALAND'S INDEPENDENT DUTCH NEWSPAPER

From our archives.

This month it will be exactly 25 years ago that the N.Z. Netherlands Society 'Oranje' Inc. committed plagiarism and also started publishing a Windmill Post.

In their wisdom the 'Oranje Society' broke off a binding contract, dumped Louis Kuys as secretary and also cancelled his wife and children's membership.

Until today these wrong doings by de Oranje Socity have never been rectified!

SUPREME COURT
COURT OF APPEAL
ALSO PRIVY COUNCIL
UPHELD OUR CLAIM TO
NAME, "WINDMILL POST"

The Solicitors were:
For the Plaintiffs
Mr R. A. Heron of Swan Davies & McKay, Wellington, for Mr L.C. Kuys and Windmill Post
For the Defendants
Mr B. H. Clark and Mr W. M. Marsh of Earl Kent Massey Palmer & Hamer, Auckland, for N.Z. Netherlands Society "Oranje"

Witnesses for Windmill Post were:
Mr L.C. Kuys, Plaintiff and Editor Windmill Post
Mr D. Ingebre ex-President of the Rotorua Club.
Mr H. Zeeman, ex-President of the Hamilton Club, and Chairman at the Delegates National Council Meeting in March 1967
Mr H.P. Willemsen, ex-publisher of the N.Z. Hollander.
Mr H. Hoebergs, member
Mr I. Griffiths, Director

Witnesses for Netherlands Society "Oranje" were:
Mr L. Renneberg, Defendant and member
Mr P. Dulcos, President Oranje Society
Miss N. Leeuman, Treasurer
Mr W. van Dongen, Manager for K.LM
Mr E. Prentice, Manager for C.P. Air
Mrs A. Hopman, member
Mr F. van Impelen, Printer of Impex Press

In a reserved judgment in the Supreme Court in Auckland His Honour Mr J. Speight said amongst other things:

"The Plaintiffs, Mr Kuys and the Windmill Post, Orange Society, to prevent the extraordinary situation whereby two almost identical newspapers are published by rival organisations. There is no doubt that Mr Kuys initiated the publication of the paper, invented its title and elected to use the windmill devices.

After six months, the Defendant, The Orange Society, also launched a similar publication and deliberately copied the Plaintiff's format and the two papers are circulating simultaneously — only distinguished by sub-headings — one of which (the Plaintiff's) claims to be an 'Independent' paper and the other claims to be the official organ of the Orange Society.

I do not find Mr Kuys at fault in any relevant matter. The conflict between these two parties is crying out for a remedy one way or the other and in my view Mr Kuys has established his case.

I hold that the paper and its title are the Plaintiff's property."

And in conclusion, the judge said:
"Accordingly, there is an injunction restraining the Defendant by itself or its agents, from publishing, distributing or selling a newspaper under the name or style of The Windmill Post or any one of the words "Windmill" or "Post" or from the use of the large windmill device on the front page."

The Orange Society took the case to the Court of Appeal in Wellington which in April 1971 upheld the judgement of the Supreme Court. The three judges (P. North, J. Turner, J. Haslam), of the Court of Appeal said amongst other things:
"The members of the Court of Appeal being unanimously of the opinion that the appeal fails, it is dismissed accordingly."

Despite the unanimous decision by the Court of Appeal the Orange Society decided to take the case to the highest possible court under the British law system: the Privy Council.
The hearing took place in London at the Privy Council on 22nd, 23rd and 24th of January 1973 before the Lords (Wilberforce, Hodson, Pearson, Diplock and Simon of Glaisdale) of the Judicial

Committee of the Privy Council delivered their judgement on March 7, 1973 upholding the decisions of the Supreme Court in Auckland and the Court of Appeal in Wellington.
The Judges of the Privy Council summed up the case finally in the following terms:
"In their Lordships opinion the injunction granted should be upheld.
Their Lordships will humbly advise Her Majesty that the appeal be dismissed. The appellant (Orange Society) must pay the cost of the appeal."

After seven years of litigations and thousands of dollars of costs to the Orange Society the name 'Windmill Post' remains rightfully ours.

To all those many people who have remained loyal to this newspaper and also to our growing number of NEW subscribers, we say a simple but sincere THANK YOU

Plagiarism fails OK!

Plagiarism rules OK?

New World Netherlanders

In its early colonial years of the 17th century, the New World of North America opened its arms to the Dutch nation. This gloriously unspoiled and uncivilized land was badly in need of an injection of tulips and Calvinism, and who better to give it to 'em than the Dutch.

The colony of New Netherland covered most of the now densely-populated northeast corridor of the United States, starting in 1609. There were many encounters, both friendly and violent, with the Indians ("Native Americans"). Many settlements were wiped out, and often the Hollanders massacred the natives. Immigration to Canada began much later (1890's) and occurred at a much slower pace.

Early colonial achievements included ~~Abel Tasman's~~ (sorry) Peter Stuyvesant's heroic loss of New Amsterdam to the English in 1664. (Unbeknownst to Stuyvesant, the two countries were at war at the time, so when an English naval vessel sailed into the harbour, Peter rushed to greet them, whereupon he was immediately fired and the place was renamed New York.) As the area was originally purchased from natives for blankets, kettles and trinkets worth all of HFl 60-, the affair was an overwhelming financial disaster as well as an embarrassment. (Although the area was reconquered in 1673, it was permanently GIVEN to England a year later.) Peter has subsequently tried to rehabilitate himself among his countrymen by using cigarette packaging to advertise himself as the *"founder"* of New York. Some links to New York's Dutch heritage are still present (for example, the present suburb of Brooklyn derives from the earlier village name ***Breuckelen***), although much has been corrupted by the overbearing English inheritance.

Holland's most identifiable contribution to the emergent continent, however, can be felt this day in the State of Michigan where large concentrations of first- through fourth-generation Dutch-Americans (the *MichiDutch*) have inhabited the picturesque landscape and infested it with tulips, (mock) windmills and other Dutch structures. (The more famous *"Pennsylvania Dutch"* are not Dutch descendants at all, but German – an example of history's corruption of *"Deutsch"* into *"Dutch."*)

Unlike the *Dutch* Dutch, the *MichiDutch* haven't changed much over the past 150+ years. They deserted their lowland-land to escape the then progressive penchant of the Dutch Reformed Church. As staunch churchgoers and moralistic merchants, they believe they are THE true Dutch. In the same way that Californian vineyards claim their *Sauterne, Cabernet Sauvignon* and *Pinot Noir* to be more French than the French varieties, the *MichiDutch* perceive themselves to be superior stock to European *cloggies*. They do not merely think that they are better than the *Dutch* Dutch – they KNOW they are better. Thus, we have the curious phenomenon of:

The Dutch above the Dutch
disowning the Dutch Dutch.

The elders of the region are embarrassed by many of the current *Dutch* Dutch traits and customs. As one *Michi-Dutch* businessman advised us, *'We're conservative here. In Holland they don't give a hoot about their image. We don't want to make that impression here.''* Many of the second- or later-generation Dutch in Western Michigan have little or no idea what the real Holland is like. They are appalled to discover what the natives (the Dutch *"over there"*) wear (or don't wear) at the beach and at the "window shopping" in certain cities in Holland. At home, they view Dutchness only from within their safe cliques and prefer to marry others of Dutch descent.

The younger variety are protected against their origins and fed on the heavenly dreams of their fathers. When they peel away from their paternal protection and venture out into the real world, the bubble bursts. Those who escape the strict community and become more Americanized would at times rather claim to be Zildenavian (see page 95) than to admit their Dutch background (variation on the theme of Dutch disowning the Dutch). Most second or subsequent generation Dutch tend to shed their *Michi-Dutch*ness once they leave their sacred pastures.

On the move again (guess where?)

Canadians have a similar situation with their Calvinist Dutch who retain many of the old practices and traits of their ancestors. They are rather conspicuous to outsiders through their churches:

> *In one small town there are five, six, or even seven such churches close to each other, and each one holds to a slightly different belief, so that they are all at odds.*
> Janny Lowensteyn (Quebec)

The rest of the New World Netherlanders have integrated to the point that they are hardly visible, although they still observe the Americans and Canadians through their original moral eyeglasses. They view their hosts as somewhat slow, "laid-back" and passive, traits which the Dutch find to be irritating: *"They never seem to protest, but just accept most things,"* complain the *cloggies* as they themselves abandon the protest practice.

In general, Americans are perceived to be more "open" than Canadians, but not nearly as "open" as Hollanders.

> *It is hard to get close to Canadians because they are reserved. They are always helpful in emergencies, but then they go back in their shell and want to be private. We Dutch are very open and ALWAYS ready with comments, criticism and advice. We're not afraid to come straight out and ask, "How much money do you make?" The Canadians think we are rude for this.*

Newcomers go through the usual frustration and comedy of adjusting to a new mentality and to different customs, as exemplified by one such immigrant:

> *The first time my wife had to go to a doctor, she was told to undress in a little room and to wait until the doctor would come. Although she noticed those gowns*

in the room, she did not put one on. (Nobody told her
about them . . .) When the doctor came in, he was quite
shocked that she was lying there au naturel.
A friend of ours was told to put one of those gowns on,
but she thought that it would be more practical for it to
be open at the front instead of the back. . . Again, that
doctor probably thought that most Dutch women are so
liberated that they do not mind to walk around naked!

Those Hollanders who elect to ride Bicycles find themselves part of a Brave New World. *"People dress up in*
special outfits, helmets, etc., like they are going to the Tour de
France. They are over-concerned about safety and liability."
The gear is ridiculous -- and even worse, it is EXPENSIVE.

The Dutch who emigrate to the New World are relieved
to find that the taxes are not nearly as high as in Holland.
While enjoying the relatively low tax rates, they strongly
criticize the sometimes tragic events that (in part) stem
from this. One especially exciting tax break exists in British
Columbia where there is no provincial sales tax on children's (under 16) clothing.

Of course, you cannot tell if a fairly large T-shirt is for
an adult or for a child. So you know what we Dutch
answer when the lady at the cash register is asking that
question!
                    Jurrian Tjeenk Willink (British Columbia)

It is easy to track Hollanders' progression across the
United States. They deposit a town called "Nederland" or
"Holland" wherever possible. "Hollands" can be found in
Massachusetts, New York, Pennsylvania, Virginia, Georgia,
Kentucky, Ohio, Michigan, Illinois, Indiana, Mississippi, Ar-
kansas, Missouri, Iowa, Minnesota, Texas and Oregon.
Canada has a few, too. There are also a fair number of

derivatives, such as Hollandale, New Holland, Holland Pond, Hollandtown, Holland Marsh and Hollandsburg.

In California, there are so many strains of lifestyle and ethnic cultural diversity (all fighting for their share of the current sensitivity and pity boom) that even the highly devout Dutch would have difficulty in raising support for Bicycle paths on freeways. Instead, they satisfy themselves by reasoning that tragedies such as the abuses of local law enforcement are none of THEIR doing – none of THEIR doing and therefore none of THEIR business. They simply go about THEIR business and occasionally spoil themselves with a personalized car licence plate or an illuminated wind-mill on the front lawn. Dutch-owned businesses often inject a bit of the old image into the thing, such as (the now defunct) Van De Kamp's Bakery in Los Angeles . . .

The Dutch influence on California architecture . . .

. . . and the Californian influence on the Dutch ego

Here is a lifestyle and mind-set as divorced from the original as the homespun *Vrouw Anje* is from those rights-swirling feminists and freedom-obsessed patriots, sliding raw fish and apple pie down their gullets, and pedaling to the bargain bread shop three miles up the road, stopping only for flowers and (free) coffee en route.

*The landscape is adversely affected by
a tall, straight dike.*
Frits Bolkestein, Dutch politician (VVD)
and philosopher, 1992.

*It is ridiculous that we have to spend so much
time talking about the struggle against water
in this modern country.*
Pieter Jan Biesheuvel, Dutch politician (CDA)
and dike specialist, 1995.

chapter 20

ANOTHER BRICK
IN THE WAAL

Dike-otomy of a Disaster

Every state has its ultimate, unthinkable disaster waiting to happen, natural or otherwise. In California, it is the *"big 'un"* earthquake that will plop half of the place into the Pacific Ocean (arguably, to the benefit of the rest of the world). In the United Kingdom, it is the destruction of the monarchy (more likely through the spread of sexually-transmitted diseases than through revolution). In Germany, it is the resurgence of Naziism. In France, it is the extinction of certain species of vegetation: the onion, the garlic clove and the grape. In Holland, it is *The Atlantis Effect*: the reclaiming of land **BY** water.

In 1995, it nearly happened -- again. In a Maginot-line scenario, the threat appeared not from the raging North Sea, but from rivers feeding the Netherlands from its neighbours: the Rhine to the east and the Maas to the south. Never before had the water in Dutch rivers been so high. A quarter of a million people were evacuated, the largest upheaval since the 1953 flood. A million cows, pigs, sheep and fowl were evacuated, as were countless Bicycles, plants, flowers and secret money stashes. A university psychologist psycho-babbled about Dutch solidarity, *". . . the element of lack of control, the feeling of the strength of nature creates a kind of solidarity."* More like plain old survival, banding together in the face of danger.

The *cloggiesque* essence of this whole event brings to mind the story of "The Hero of Haarlem," a quaint vignette included in a children's book *Hans Brinker*, by Mary Mapes Dodge, first published in the late 1800s. The "hero" is the eight-year-old son of a Haarlem sluicer. According to preposterous foreign folklore, this boy saved the entire country of Holland by plugging a dike with his little finger until help arrived the following morning, the moral of the story being that, *"Not a leak can show itself anywhere, either in its politics, honor, or public safety, that a million fingers are not ready to stop it, at any cost."* The story is neither popular nor widely known in Holland. This, then, is our updated version, which takes place in the south of the country in modern times, and incorporates real-life events from the 1995 disaster.

Hans Verdrinker

In 1995, there lived in the Land of Maas and Waal a sunny-haired boy, Hans Verdrinker, whose father was a farmer by profession and a "black" dike-*kijker* on the side. That is, he kept a watchful eye on the water levels and the condition of the double and triple river-dikes, many of which had fallen into disrepair over the years.

February 2nd was a typical day of torrential rain, and the boy put on his rain gear in order to take some space cakes to a gay couple who lived in the countryside. After spending an hour with his grateful friends, the boy started on his homeward trek. Trudging stoutly along the river, he pondered how German, French and Belgian canalisation, melting snow in the faraway Alps, and prolonged rainfall throughout northern Europe had swollen the waters. Towns in Belgium, France, Germany and Holland had been flooded. He thought about the recent voluntary evacuations from Limburg and Bommelerwaard and all the fuss and bother in his own village.

It had been painful to move the Verdrinker furniture and carpets upstairs. They had to shove and carry everything up the typical winding, narrow staircase. And his visiting *oma* made a huge fuss about saving the *vitrage* and ugly, dusty orange blinds since she had paid for them as a young wife and didn't want her fond memories washed away in a flood, although a good washing was certainly what they needed.

Hans remembered how his *opa* had bossed everyone around while having a good time doing nothing himself. *"Is there a wave coming? If only it could be a heat wave,"* he joked to one of his older friends. *"I don't want to live here anymore. I got seasick from all the water,"* his friend had joked back. And the pair knocked back some bottles of beer and smoked cigars while bragging about how hard life had been in their youth.

Hans thought of how his father had screamed at the evacuation authorities, *"I have hundreds of cows and pigs. I am staying put. You don't get me out!"* Yes, Hans felt he was indeed lucky to be part of such a cosy family. While humming his favourite street-organ medley, the boy thought of his father's moonlighting activities: *"If the dikes break, where would father and mother be? Where would the **zwart geld** be?"*

It was growing dark and he was still some distance from home. With a beating heart, he quickened his footsteps in the pouring rain. To lessen his fear, he began practicing the Dutch art of finger-pointing that had been passed down through the ages. First he rehearsed the vertical-and-oscillating manoeuvre, where the index finger points directly upwards and the forearm swings back-and-forth (to emphasise a philosophical ideal or point of view). Next he practiced the horizontal-poking manoeuvre (traditionally used during arguments). Just as he was bracing himself for a subtle manoeuvre-change, he heard the sound of trickling water. Looking up, he saw a small hole in the dike. A tiny stream was flowing through the barrier. The small hole would soon be a large one and a terrible flood would result.

When Hans leant forward to inspect the leak, his foot slipped on a damp, dank dome of dog dung. As he fell forward, his outstretched finger rammed into the hole of the failing dike, effectively sealing it. His finger was stuck solidly and the flow of water stopped. *"Zo!"* he thought, *"Another use for the eternally pointing finger of the Dutchman. And Holland will not be drowned while I am here!"*

He thought about the 100,000 people who had been evacuated from Tiel and Culemborg a few days ago and wished they could see him now. Images of metre-high inundations in Borgharen and Itteren haunted him. He was determined not to let his town be flooded (not that he had much choice in the matter).

He smiled as he thought about the prison in Maastricht that had been evacuated. The guards feared that groundwater would short circuit a computer located, of all places, in the cellar. The computer controlled the locks on cell doors and a Maas escape of prisoners was anticipated.

He was proud that his little lowland country was back in the world news, even if it was because of a disaster -- *"We count again!"* seemed to be the general gist. Most local reports were about the solidarity, bravery and generosity of the Dutch. Indeed, HFl 33 million had been collected by the **Nationaal Rampenfonds** in just one night -- big money for such a small country. But a Belgian newspaper, *De Morgen*, pointed out,

> . . . *The horror is high in the land that always thinks itself to be safe among the tulips and hashish. Proud of their dikes and their mastery over water, the illusion has now been washed away.*

Hans was determined to disprove this Flemish flotsom! And then there was that British journalist who mistranslated **kwelwater** into "torture water" -- the Brits never were very skilled when it came to foreign languages, but Hans was beginning to think that this wasn't such a bad term after all.

The boy looked up and down the dike for rescue and spotted a gaggle of his contemporaries pedalling their way down the dike. He called frantically for help. *"Kijk es! It's*

Hans. Why are you leaning on the wall, Hans? We are escaping from the evacuation. The army is chasing us. See you!" was the reply. And with that, they disappeared to the clatter of multiple rusty Bike chains.

This plunged him into a gloomy mood and soon he was thinking of stories his *opa* told him about the horrible 1953 floods that had claimed 1835 lives. Dikes in 400 locations had broken during a storm, exactly 42 years ago to the day. Hans was proud to have his finger in the dike and wished his Queen could see him.

He frowned as he thought about vandals kicking in some of the emergency dikes, resulting in all-night patrols by beefy farm women armed with baseball bats in some areas. Or how about the poor saps who heard a prank radio broadcast telling them to evacuate, only to later discover their homes had been plundered during their absence.

Night fell rapidly. Our little hero shouted loudly, but no one came to his rescue. He shouted again, *"**Shit!** Will no one come? Mama! Mama!"* But, alas, his mother worried not about her son -- she respected the young boy's right to privacy. Then he called on God to consider possibly helping him, if the angelic flock agreed and there would be no *borgsom* involved. The answer came, through a holy resolution, *"When I am rescued, I will charge the Rijkswaterstaat a dike-kijker's fee, plus a HFl 500- bonus for temporary repairs!"* And with that, he fell into an uncomfortable sleep leaning against the rain-soaked dike.

Hans awoke the next morning to the familiar sound of mooing, belching, flatulating cows. *"Mama, papa, you have saved me,"* he mumbled hoarsely, for he had lost his voice in the damp, cold night. As he peered over the dike, he saw a strange sight -- barges of cows being transported to safety. *"Godverdomme!"* he thought, *"I must be hallucinating for lack of food. What I wouldn't give for a soggy uitsmijter!"*

A loud ruckus nearby suddenly caught his attention as an army patrol vehicle came to a halt along the dike. It was the platoon commander, a long-haired, lanky lad from Friesland, assigned to the area. Our young hero could hear loud voices in the distance as the commander spoke with some townsfolk who were debating whether to evacuate or stay put. *"In my mind, the situation is not life threatening here. As far as I'm concerned, you can just stay,"* said the commander.

In the meantime, his squad of soldiers was building an emergency dike with sandbags. Hans heard both laughing and complaining emanating from the ranks. *"It's hard work, filling up the sandbags, and long hours. We must talk to the union about this,"* was the crux of the complaints. Hans learned that each bag weighed about 15 kilos, so in one day, several thousand kilos would pass through each soldier's soiled, sweaty hands. *"The coordination and safety aren't the best. It's good that the work inspectors can't see this. Ha ha,"* was one of the jokes Hans could hear. The exercise was very important for the townspeople, since word had reached them that Heerewaarden was charging HFl 5- for a solitary sandbag, instead of issuing them free.

The commander and residents were still discussing matters when the mayor suddenly arrived on his Bicycle. *"What are you doing here? All you people have to evacuate immediately!"* he bellowed. *"Ja, but the mobile unit doesn't agree,"* replied the commander. The mayor burst into anger and retorted, *"The mobile unit is completely wrong. Everyone has to get out. It's time for the mobile unit, police, volunteers, demonstrators, protesters, environmentalists, fire-*

men, farmers, Vrouwen, flikkers, and everyone else to . . . OBEY ORDERS!" As the mayor and the military squabbled over power, the townsfolk quietly slipped away to carry on with their lives: the concept of "orders," and the obeying of them, was something they would rather not contemplate.

In the end, the mayor won, as evidenced by a stream of traffic crawling slowly across the distant bridge later that morning. Hans recognized people from his own town in what looked like an endless gypsy caravan, with furniture, suitcases, Bicycles, chickens, toys, pets and potted plants stuffed in cars, trucks, tractors and buses, or piled high on the roofs of the vehicles. The ever-present wind shifted direction and Hans heard the angry voice of a neighbour exclaim, *"Unbelievable! We are fleeing for our lives, yet we still have to pay the toll for crossing the stupid bridge!"* Everyone was leaving while Hans the saviour was stuck in the source of the scourge.

A rustling noise at his feet startled him, and he looked down in dismay. A rabbit was tunneling into the dike that he was trying to save! *"Sodemieter op!"* he croaked at the creature, wondering what he could use to plug this potential breach. Just the other day, he had seen a group of men from the Royal Hunters Association paddling around in boats, trying to rescue rabbits and other wild creatures from various dry havens such as trees, so they could hunt and shoot the critters after the flood.

His thoughts turned again to the evacuations. In Gameren, 40 gardeners had remained in their nursery, refusing to move. On the island of Nederhemert, everyone remained at home. Even the replacement dike master of Groot Maas en Waal stubbornly stayed on evacuated territory. So why was Hans so alone now? He thought that maybe it was the dreaded **Mobiele Eenheid** (mobile military patrol) that was responsible for his isolation. Typically, fugitives were collected by such patrols and escorted to emergency relief camps -- a few hours later, many would be back home again, having escaped from the confines of safety. He comforted himself with the thought that maybe help would arrive after all.

Visions of evacuating the pigs and cows from his father's farm were vivid. Before the evacuation, Hans had no idea how sensitive to stress and disease pigs were. Although moving the animals had taken a whole day -- some had left in trucks, others on the train -- it had not been the most organized move in Dutch history. Many farmers had no idea where their livestock had been relocated to, the animals had no idea where they were, and some recipients had no idea where their new charges came from. Other concerned citizens had graciously offered asylum for snakes, spiders, rats and other cuddly *cloggy* pets.

In his moments of boredom, Hans tried to envision life in one of the (free) relief camps. He had seen people interviewed on TV who reported that life was generally quite acceptable there. At one camp housing 1,300 evacuees, most thought that things were fine. *"They've thought of everything here. It's a bit like being on vacation,"* said one of the evacuees at the camp. The more enterprising inmates sifted through evacuated insurance papers, purchase receipts and bank statements, and spent their days calculating how best to capitalise on the calamity.

Yet this would not be Holland without some whinging and whining. One woman grumbled to reporters that her knitting had been left behind and she did not want to spend money on more wool when she had some floating around in her home. To some evacuees, snoring was the main nightmare. *"The neighbour to my left snores, the guy behind me snores, and the neighbour to my right coughs all night long. This is no party. Everything is well taken care of, but I can't last much longer,"* said a resident of Zaltbommel. One man staying at an antique car museum couldn't take it any longer and sought refuge in a soundproof ice cream truck. The whole concept started to sound like luxury to Hans.

The sound of a boat engine rescued the boy from his thoughts, but alas not from his situation. He peered over the top of the dike and couldn't believe his eyes. There they were, boatloads of gaping disaster-tourists. They were smiling, waving and snapping photos of him as they sailed past, having paid HFl 6,50 each for the tour. As bad luck would have it, our hero could not scream for help.

Then something so extraordinary and wonderful happened that Hans ceased feeling sorry for himself for a few moments. The event happened when he noticed the daytrippers gather on one side of the boat, madly waving, jumping up and down, yelling, and generally making even bigger fools of themselves. He turned to see what could cause them to act so apelike when he suddenly saw lots of TV cameras and the whole media circus swarming along the dike about a kilometre away. The next thing he knew, he saw his beloved Queen, hatless and decked in rubber boots and raincoat, stomping through the mud to survey the flood damage. It was a moment Hans would never forget. Unfortunately, the entourage was headed away from him.

Hans consoled himself by daydreaming about meeting his Queen. Later that day, a defiant environmentalist who had refused to leave the town was walking along the top of Hans' dike, allowing his dog to fertilise the cycle path in the traditional Dutch manner. The environmentalist heard our hero groaning. Expecting to rescue a small, furry animal in distress, he bent down and discovered the weak and hungry child. With disappointment, he bellowed, *"**Godverdomme!** What are you doing there?"* Hans cleared his sore throat and gave the simple, yet honest answer, *"I am keeping the water from running out, you **klootzak!**"* then added, for effect, *"Send for help. We must shore up the dike."*

"No way!" the environmentalist replied logically, *"The town is deserted now. Besides, if I do that, the authorities will come later and build all kinds of ugly new dikes and emergency water walls that cause visual pollution. Ja! They might even erect some of those ugly new wind generators that don't look anything like our lovely picture-postcard windmills. That's horizon pollution!"*

"I haven't had my morning bread yet," the boy pleaded, *"do you have any?"* *"Better than that, here –"* the environmentalist replied as he threw the boy a small bag of muesli and pointed to some dandelion leaves growing just out of reach. *"You should really consider fasting instead of eating everyday. This way you can purify your body. Well, I must leave now to kick a few dikes!"* was his parting gesture.

So there the boy remained for yet another night, thanks to his enviro-animal-rights friend. It was only the thoughts of humbly recounting his adventures on NED-2, BRT1 & 2, ZDF, BBC and CNN (and the **geld** that could be gained) that shored up our hero this second night. Where were the stampeding media hordes? If only they would pass by, he could sign autographs and perhaps even a book contract.

As daylight came the following morning, the environmentalist returned with others of his ilk, and they had heated discussions and debates about all things and theories environmental, again ignoring tired and hungry Hans. *"It is mankind and greedy polititians that are to blame for the rape of the Rhine. We have been raping nature for 40 years,"* said one of the caring crowd. *"Yes! Nature is showing us this was wrong,"* declared another. All the green guys agreed that they were being unfairly blamed for the floods, even though they were partly responsible. True, they had prevented strengthening and extending the dikes for many years with their protests, but all they wanted was to preserve the Rembrandt landscape. Now everyone was mad at them. It was unfair because the politicians were already using the floods as political fodder for elections. After some hours of debate, the environmentalists departed for more debate and *inspraakprocedures*, leaving Hans behind once again, and giving him the distinct impression that these floods were simply just the result of too much talk.

Then something really fantastic and unusual happened, and it cheered up Hans immensely. The sun came out! *"JA, JA, JA! This is an important sign. Now I know I'll be saved,"* he thought.

And he was right. Later that day, he saw mobs of people dancing on the dike and returning home. Horns were blaring, but not from joy -- everyone was furious at the long lines of traffic. Hans heard a busload of impatient inebriated locals screaming that the return home was more of a disaster than the evacuation and that they should somehow be compensated for both. He wondered why the drivers were all making a huge detour instead of taking the direct route across the bridge. Later, he learned it was to avoid paying the bridge toll again.

Our hero, a bit thinner for his ordeal, was eventually discovered by some returning farmers, who found his tale most incredible. A few minutes later, the local chapter of greenies returned to the scene, having at last found a solution to the problem of the deserted digit in the dike. Despite the experiences of the past week, the townspeople accepted the green-team dike-mender's credentials and noticably subdued rantings about *"nature's way of objecting"* and humanity having *"no right to impose its hedonist . . . blah, blah."* With that, the farmers all wished the boy a speedy recovery, and left to find their cows, pigs and chickens, and to buy more batteries for their calculators (which were sure to work overtime in the ensuing months, considering that many of the recently repatriated were protesting, filing lawsuits and making major money machinations about their flood losses). The sight of at least five zeroes lined up before the decimal point brought some to the brink of orgasm.

Then suddenly, without a word of warning or regret, the dike mender, with one swoop of his axe, divorced the boy from the barrier, close to the knuckle. In one motion, he had permanently plugged the leak, aesthetically appeased the green team, saved the son from starvation . . . and also stopped the kid from picking his nose and making his point! In future debates, when people would pontificate, *"There was no disaster, there was only high water,"* or *"The '95 floods caused inconvenience, not a disaster,"* there would be at least one hero, Hans Verdrinker, who could prove, with one hand raised, that indeed there had been a disaster, though now part of him was . . .

"JUST ANOTHER BRICK IN THE WAAL."

appendices

APPENDIX A
A View of the Dutch
through the
English Language

APPENDIX B
A Chosen Selection of
Dutch/English Homonyms

APPENDIX C
In Case You Don't Believe Us . . .

APPENDIX A

A View of the Dutch through the English Language

Dutch angle	in cinematography, a shot in which the camera is tilted to intentionally distort or disorientate.
Dutch auction	an auction that proceeds backwards; one in which the price is reduced until a buyer is found.[2]
Dutch bargain	bargain made and sealed while drinking.[3]

beat the **Dutch**	to do something extraordinary or startling. Ex: How does he do it? It beats the Dutch.[1]
Dutch built	originally, Dutch flat-bottomed vessels;[1] current usage attibuted to (a) male: long and lanky (b) female: see "Dutch buttocked."
Dutch buttocked	originally, a strain of Dutch cattle with large hind quarters;[1] contemporary association is the large, pear-shaped rump of modern Dutch women, stemming from excessive bicycle riding and dairy products.
Dutch concert	babble of noises.[5]
Dutch consolation	the philosophy or attitude that, "Whatever ill befalls you, there is someone worse off than you."[1]
Dutch courage	courage induced by alcoholic drink.[2]
Dutch defence	surrender.[5]
do a **Dutch**	to desert, escape; to commit suicide.[1]
double **Dutch**	gibberish.[1]
dutching	the use of gamma rays to make spoiled food edible again.[4]
dutchman	an object for hiding faulty workmanship (construction).
Dutch feast	a party where the entertainer gets drunk before his guests.[1]
Dutch gleek	heavy or excessive drinking.
go **Dutch**	to have each person pay his own expenses.

(I'm a) **Dutch**man	a phrase implying refusal or disbelief.[2]
in **Dutch**	in disfavour, disgrace or trouble.[1]
Dutch it	double-cross.
Dutch lottery	a lottery in which tickets are drawn in certain classes or series for each of which certain prizes increasing in number and value with each class are fixed.[3]
Dutch metal	a malleable alloy . . . beaten into thin leaves and used as cheap imitation of gold-leaf; also called "Dutch gold," "Dutch foil" and "Dutch leaf." [1]
Dutch nightingale	a frog.
Dutch oven	a person's mouth.[1]
Dutch reckoning	guesswork.
to **Dutch**	to miscalculate in placing bets so as to have a mathematical expectancy of losing rather than winning.[3]
Dutch treat	a party, outing, etc. at which each participant pays for his own share (corruption of "Dutch trait").[2]
Dutch uncle	a severe critic or counsellor.
Dutch widow	prostitute.[5]

---

1 The Oxford Dictionary, Clarendon Press, 1989, Vol. IV, p. 1140-1141.

2 The Oxford Reference Dictionary, Clarendon Press, 1986, p. 253.

3 By permission. From Webster's Third New International Dictionary
   © 1986 by Merriam-Webster Inc., publisher of the Merriam-Webster® dictionaries.

4 Volkskrant, July 1990.

5. Archaic.

APPENDIX B

A Chosen Selection of Dutch/English Homonyms

Incorrect use of Dutch/English homonyms can have an interesting effect on people. At an informal get-together, one Dutch woman introduced herself to a British woman. When asked about her profession, the Dutch woman calmly replied, *"I fuck dogs."*

Here are some of the more potentially disastrous cases:

Dutch – English

Dutch word	Sounds like	Dutch word means
dik	dick	fat, thick
doop	dope	baptize
douche	douche	shower
fiets	feats	bicycle
fok	fuck	breed
heet	hate	to be named
hoor	whore	hear
kaak	cock	jaw
kip	kip	chicken
kont	cunt	buttocks
krap	crap	skint, penniless
kwik	quick	mercury
ledikant	lady can't	bed
mais	mice	corn
meet	mate	mark, measure
mes	mess	knife
peen	pain	carrot
pieper	peeper	potato
prik	prick	tonic water
reep	rape	rope, line
rente	rent	account, interest
sectie	sexy	section
shag	shag	cigarette tobacco
snoep	snoop	sweets, candy
toneel	toenail	theatre, play
vaart	fart	travel, sail
vlaai	fly	fruit pie, tart
winkel	winkle	shop

English – Dutch

English word	Sounds like	Dutch word means
Bic	*bik*	to screw, fuck
bill	*bil*	buttock
brill(iant)	*bril*	glasses, toilet seat
coke	*kook*	cook
cut	*kut*	vagina, cunt
dear	*dier*	animal
dote	*dood*	dead
flicker	*flikker*	homosexual, gay
freight	*vreet*	to eat (of animals)
fry	*vrij*	free (vulg. fuck)
lull	*lul*	penis
novel	*navel*	navel
paper	*peper*	pepper
peace, piece	*pies*	piss
pick	*pik*	penis
pimple	*pimpel*	boozing
rate	*reet*	backside, arse
ritz	*rits*	zipper
slim	*slim*	clever
slip	*slip*	underpants
slope	*sloop*	wreck, pillowcase
Spain	*speen*	nipple
steak	*steek*	stab
tipple	*tippel*	streetwalk (whore)

APPENDIX C

In Case You Don't Believe Us

Apartheid is Deservedly a Dutch Word	*NRC Handelsblad,* 1 September 1992.
A Brief Character of the Low-Countries . . .	*Owen Feltham,* London, 1652.
The Corner Hashish Joint	*Los Angeles Times,* December 10, 1992. p. E1.
Council has to Finance Sex Grant	*The Times,* 25 July, 1992.

Cruise Missile Protest	*Aviation Week & Space Technology,* September 30, 1985, p. 79.
Doing Time the Dutch Way	*World Press Review,* May 1988, p. 53.
Draagbaar Homomonument (Portable Homo-Monument)	*de Volkskrant,* 24 November 1988.
The Dutch Dole	*Art in America,* July 1990, p. 83-85.
The Dutch Touch	*National Geographic,* October 1986, p. 501-525.
Dutch Treat	*Forbes,* July 2, 1985, p. 31.
The Embarrassment of Riches	*Simon Schama,* New York, 1987.
Europe's Least Awful Prisons (Dutch Jails)	*The Economist,* February 6, 1988, p. 17-19.
Everyday Racism (Alledaags Racisme)	*Philomena Essed* California, USA, 1990.
Flower Power: Everything's Coming up Tulips in the Netherlands	*Newsweek,* May 5, 1986, p. 42-43.
Geen Zuivere Koffee (No Real Coffee)	*Algemeen Dagblad,* 8 November 1989, p.17.
The Great Dutch Recycling Farce	*New Scientist,* February 2, 1992, p. 49-50.
The Great Landfall Controversy or Where Was Abel on 13th December in 1642	*de Oranje Wimpel,* Issue 68, April, 1992, p. 13-14.
Hans Brinker or The Silver Skates	*Mary Mapes Dodge,* New York, 1875.

Holland: Drawing the Line, Has Permissiveness Gone Too Far?	*Time,* August 10, 1987 (European edition), p. 18-24.
Holland Suffers From an Acute Case of Eurosclerosis	*Business Month,* March 1989, p. 30-31.
Hollanditis: A New Stage in European Neutralism	*Commentary,* August 1981, p. 19-26.
Institutional Tolerance of Marijuana in Holland	*Whole Earth Review,* Spring 1987, p. 58-59.
Is it Time to Build Another Ark?	*U.S. News,* November 20, 1989, p. 12.
A Load of . . . (Mountains of Manure in the Netherlands)	*The Economist,* March 14, 1987, p. 46.
Miljiard Gulden Omzet in Sekshuizen (Billion Guilder Brothel Business)	*de Hollandse Krant,* 25 October 1992.
Money Seems to Grow on Tulips	*Fortune,* October 12, 1987, p. 180-181.
Moving the Mud	*Scientific American,* March 1982, p. 76.
Plenty of Let and Hindrance	*The Economist,* September 17, 1988, p. 53.
The Pomp and the Protest	*Newsweek,* May 12, 1980, p. 73.
The Pope on Hostile Soil	*Newsweek,* May 13, 1985, p. 35.
The Pope's Dutch Welcome	*Newsweek,* May 27, 1985, p. 8-10.

Pulling in the Welcome Mat: Protests and Slim Turnouts Mar John Paul's Dutch Visit	*Time,* May 27, 1985, p. 64-65.
Rebates on Rubbish	*New Scientist,* December 1, 1990, p. 26.
Saying it with Flowers	*The Economist,* January 10, 1987, p. 55.
Shrewd Managers of Regal Riches	*Fortune,* October 12, 1987, p. 134-35.
Tolerance Finally Finds Its Limits	*Time,* August 31, 1987 (USA edition), p. 28-29.
Too Good to Last (Dutch welfare benefits)	*The Economist,* March 30, 1985, p. 62-63.
Watersnood 1995 (1995 Flood - National Action Book)	*Inmerk b.v.,* 1995.
Watersnood 1995 (1995 Flood - The Dutch Had to Unite ... a bit)	*Sijthoff Pers b.v.,* 1995.
The War on Plant Theft	*Maclean's,* June 10, 1985, p. 65-66.
Where the 60's Never Ended	*New York Times Magazine,* October 20, 1985, p. 28-37.
Windmills and Warheads	*America,* June 20, 1981, p. 494.

index

A

Aalsmeer 39, 41
Abortion. 99, 133, 181
Afrikaans 155, 210
Afrikaners. 209-212
AIDS 125, 154
Aktie
   See Campaigns
Alkmaar 188
Amstelveen. 41
Amsterdam. 1, 11, 20, 24, 34, 41, 49, 60,
                      90, 92, 98-100, 103, 122, 137,
                      140, 152-153, 179, 185, 187, 189
Anti-Nuclear 96
Apartheid. 122, 210-212
Appeal 93-95

Architecture 24-26, 202, 205-207, 225
Arnhem 184
Aruba. 205, 208
Australia. 194, 212-215
Axioms
    Debate 93
    Dutch above the Dutch 221
    Dutch Language. 156
    Early bird. 78
    Elderly Drivers 114
    Freebies 71
    Houses (size of) 24
    Law of Motion 20
    Marriage and Money. 128
    National Nature (retention of). 197
    Road Rights. 115
    Woman's Freedom 183
    Woman's Right 104

B

Banks. 68-69, 206
Banners 91
Bartering 10, 63, 65-66, 72, 112
Beer. 171-172, 191, 197-199,
                                                                215-216, 230
Beschuit met muisjes. 172, 174
Bicycle. 8, 16, 24-25, 37, 52, 100, 111,
                                            139-143, 162, 178, 181, 203,
                                            224-225, 228, 232-234
Birthdays 63, 77, 135-136
Bloemen
    See Flowers
Bloemencorso 41
Boer. 209
Bommelerwaard 229
Borgharen. 231
Borgsom 111, 232
Brabant 156, 164
Brazil 2, 208
Buttons, campaign. 90-92, 97

C

Calvinism 29, 73-74, 180, 202, 204, 208,
                                                                220, 223

Campaigns 63, 94, 96-97, 100, 152, 184
Camping. 125-126
Canada. 194, 220, 223-224
Canals 6, 9, 35, 145, 161, 206
Catholicism. 133-134, 202, 221
Causes. 89, 95-98, 122, 169
Children
    As gods 48, 50
    Behaviour 43, 49-55, 109, 112, 126, 149
    Schooling 49, 52-53
    See also Vandalism
Christmas. 63, 137-138, 149, 206
Cinema. 50, 57-60
Cleanliness 10, 169
Climate 8, 136, 146, 203
Coffee 33, 45, 72, 74, 77, 81, 126,
                    129-133, 135-136, 169, 176, 188,
                    202, 204, 207-208, 226
Cohabitating 128
Complain 15, 18, 89, 93, 108-109, 149,
                    188, 202, 207, 233, 235
Computers 19, 68, 70-71, 231
Cows. 43, 45-46, 228, 230, 232, 235, 239
Crime. 64, 88, 122, 180, 184, 188-189
Culemborg 231
Currency
    See Guilder
Curtains 29, 229

D

Demonstrations. 20, 77, 89, 96-97, 99, 134,
                    144, 146, 152-153, 202
Den Haag
    See The Hague
Dikes 6, 9, 124, 139, 144-145, 161,
                    194, 227-239
Discussion & Debate 89, 92-93, 144-146, 153, 170,
                    188, 233-234, 237-238
Dish Washing
    See Washing Dishes
Divorce 99, 133
Driving. 8, 113-118
Driving Licence 117-118, 206

Dropjes 174-175, 202
Drugs. 20, 22, 64, 104, 122, 137, 179,
185-188, 190-191, 231
Dutch
  See also Appendices
  Auction. 39
  Character 7-10, 231
  Colonies 194, 204-209, 220
  Democracy 15, 68, 96, 115
  Dozen. 109
  Future. 54-55
  Gable 25, 35, 202, 207, 225
  Immodesty 180-181
  Language 1, 59, 124, 155-162, 171, 203,
206, 213
  Overseas. 2, 193-226
  Reputation. 7-10, 121, 185
  Sign Language 114, 127, 230
  Staircase. 24, 27, 35, 229
  Way 98-99, 135, 217
Dutch/English Homonyms. 247-249

E

Egmond 150-152
Eindhoven. 22, 143
Environmentalists 2, 233, 236-239

F

Feminism
  See *Vrouwen*
Fines 16, 66-68
Flag, Dutch
  See Patriotism
Flea Market. 112, 136
Flessenlikker 177-178
Flood 227-239
Floriade 40-41
Flowers 16, 37-43, 48, 72, 81, 135, 141,
162, 169, 200-201, 226, 228, 231
Food 6, 45, 163-176, 197, 202,
205-206, 226
Foreigners. 7, 76, 84
Friesland. 157, 233
Funerals 72

Furnishings 28-29, 33, 35
Future 54-55

G

Gameren 234
Gezellig 23, 202
Goodbyes 125, 136
Graffiti 88, 90
Greetings 135
Groningen 154, 156-157, 194, 214
Groot Maas en Waal 234
Grootegast 213-214
Guilder
  As Currency 10, 40, 61-73, 95-96, 108-109,
                                          135, 169-170, 182, 203, 220,
                                                   231, 233, 237-238
  As Deity 15, 18, 41, 51, 61, 65, 69, 73,
                                          78, 107, 112, 114, 128, 139, 182,
                                                   195, 197, 202, 234-235, 239

H

Haarlem 228
Hallo 51, 159
Handshake 124-125, 135-136
Haring 172-173
Health Care 76-77, 82, 154, 182
Heerewaarden 233
Herring
  See *Haring*
Hilversum 12
Home 23-38, 176
Homosexual
  Gay 20, 96, 103, 140, 152-153, 179
  Lesbian 96, 152
  Monument 153
Homosexuality, in general 99, 123, 127, 133, 153
House Pets 16, 23, 34, 188, 234-235
House Plants 23, 28, 30, 33, 38, 41-42,
                                                   126, 142, 169, 228, 234
Houseboats 34-36
Housing 90, 98

I

Ice Skating 52, 69, 145
Icons 196
Identification Papers. 84, 123
Idioms 78, 81, 160-162, 243-244
Indonesia 2, 121, 204-205
Initials, signing of 83-85
Introductions. 86, 135
Itteren 231

K

Kitchen 33-34, 176-178
Koekjes 72, 176, 202
Krakers 20, 29, 98

L

Leiden 123
Liberation Day. 138
Limburg 229
Loosdrecht 12

M

Maas and Waal 229
Maastricht 231
Manners. 8, 17-20, 37, 58-59, 86-88,
                                     108-112, 114, 124-125, 195
Manure 42-43
Marijuana
  See Drugs
Marriage. 127-129
Maxims
  See Axioms
MichiDutch. 221-223
Michigan, USA
  See MichiDutch
Midwives 48
Military Service 103-106, 232-235
Money
  See Guilder
Moroccans 53, 103, 118, 122-123, 182
Music. 60, 72, 111, 134, 189-191, 230

N

Nationaal Rampenfonds 231
Nederhemert 234
Nedlanderthal Man 141
Negroes 15, 137, 208, 211-212
Netherlands Antilles 117-118, 205-208
New Year's Eve 138
New Zealand 194, 212, 216-219
Noordoostpolder 184

O

Objecting 93-95, 103

P

Paraaf
   See Initials
Patriotism 25, 92, 126, 138-140, 145-146
Personal Computers
   See Computers
Phobia
   Disgrace 25
   Sweaty Hands 124-125
   Telephone 86-88
   Threshold 107
Political Parties 6
Pope 133-135, 208
Population 1, 5
Prison 103, 188, 231
Prostitutes
   See Sex
Protest 42, 89, 93-95, 97, 103, 115,
                                            134, 144-145, 147, 182, 184,
                                            193, 202, 217, 223, 238-239
Public Transport 11-22, 143

Q

Queen's Birthday 136-137, 200, 206
Queuing 20, 68, 108

R

Racism 15, 53, 68, 76, 99, 121-123,
                                            137, 211-212
Randstad 22, 182, 185

Reclaimed Land 6, 9, 139, 144
   See also Dikes
Recycling
   See Rubbish
Red Thread (organisation) 182-183
Religion 2, 52, 128, 133-134, 202
Rijschool 117-119
Roads 8, 113, 115, 140, 206
Rock 'n Roll
   See Music
Role Reversal 128
Rotterdam 10-11, 22, 179, 191
Royalty. 90, 95, 116, 134, 139-140,
                         145-149, 158, 162, 232, 236
Rubber Stamp 84
Rubbish 58, 68, 110, 148-152

S

Sales 63, 65, 107, 110, 136
Savings Stamps. 66, 109
Scheveningen 157
Second-hand Transactions 65-66
Self-esteem 6
Servants. 137, 197
Sex
   Attitude 91, 180, 188
   Passion 180
   Prostitutes. 35, 148, 182-184, 187, 206
   Shops 6, 175, 184-185
   Toys. 181, 184
Shit 21, 42, 46, 71, 140, 174, 232
Shopping 63-64, 108-112, 189
Signature 83-85
Slogans 76-77, 90, 96, 134, 147
Snack Bars 169-170
Someren. 194
South Africa 2, 155, 194, 209-212
Sports 69-70, 126, 145
Spy Mirror 25
Squatters
   See *Krakers*
Staphorst 90
Statiegeld. 108, 110-111

Stickers, campaign 91, 100
Street Markets 6, 41, 64, 103, 112, 137, 140
Strip Ticket. 12-13
Stuyvesant, Peter 220
Subsidies 18, 42, 79-81, 98
Subtitles. 59
Supermarkets 51, 108-110, 129
Suriname 15, 103, 118, 122, 208-209

T

T-shirts, campaign. 92
Tasman, Abel 213-214, 216-217, 220
Tasmania 213-214
Tax 24, 28, 76, 79, 95-96, 113-114,
                                    128-129, 182-184, 206, 218, 224
Taxis 11, 21-22, 142
   Hasjtaxi 22
   Taxicentrale 21
   Treintaxi 22
Telephone. 65, 86-88, 100
The Hague 22, 99, 179, 182, 191, 205, 218
Tickets. 12-16
   for Bicycle Travel 16
   for Dog Travel 16
   for Queueing 68
   Parking 67
Tiel 231
Tilburg 22
Tipping. 170
Toilet. 26, 30-33, 35
Tourist Attractions. 6, 45, 139, 144, 160, 182, 185,
                                    194-195, 200, 202, 214, 217,
                                              221, 225, 237
Tourists 7, 185, 206, 209
Traffic Jams 116, 234, 238
Train Schedules. 14
Trees 26, 42-45
Tulips
   See Flowers
Turks 15, 53, 103, 118, 122-123

U

Uitkering
   See Welfare

USA. 45, 194, 220-226
Utrecht. 35, 96

V

Van Diemen, Anthony 213
Vandalism. 43, 88, 149
Verhoeven, Paul 60, 193
Verzuiling 153
Volendam. 156
Vrouwen 20, 99-104, 128, 134, 152,
                                              181, 183, 226, 234

W

Washing Dishes. 176-177
Welfare 2, 18, 53, 75-82, 100, 122,
                                                      128, 152
Windmills
  See Tourist Attractions
Windows 25-26, 28-30
  Cleaning 26, 29
Women
  See *Vrouwen*
Wooden Shoes 6, 43, 45, 64, 160, 194-195,
                                              206, 212
Work 77-79, 81
  Benefits 77, 103, 127
  Dismissal from 78-79
  Holidays 81, 103, 127, 195, 206
  Sick Leave. 81
  See also Welfare

Z

Zaltbommel. 236
Zapping. 53
Zeedijk. 187
Zwart (black)
  Piet. 137, 206
  Travel. 15-16
  Work 76, 229-230

about the authors

Colin White was born in Windsor, England. He has worked extensively in Europe, primarily as a technical writer in the aerospace industry. In 1979 he moved to Holland to assist with the production of aircraft maintenance documentation for the Dutch aircraft manufacturer Fokker. He remained for a total of seven years, residing in Amstelveen, Amsterdam, Huizen, Hilversum and Loosdrecht. He moved to California in mid 1987 to pursue other interests.

Laurie Boucke was born in Oakland, California, and studied languages at the University of California in the USA and also at the University of Grenoble in France. She moved frequently throughout western Europe, eastern Europe and the subcontinent of India. She was a resident of the Netherlands for 15 years, living mainly in Amsterdam and Alkmaar. She raised three children in the Dutch environment. Laurie returned to her native California in early 1987.

Since adopting domicile in the USA, Colin and Laurie have together founded WHITE-BOUCKE PUBLISHING, a company specializing in industrial and legal documentation. The UnDutchables formed their first foray into the commercial publishing market.

GENERAL NON-FICTION TITLES

A JOURNEY BETWEEN SOULS (Elaine Edgar)

Biography of Richard Adamson, the British soldier who provided security for Howard Carter's expedition when Tutankhamun's tomb was found. Discover the truth about the find, the curse, and the man who slept alone in the tomb for seven years! Available late 1996, ISBN 1-888580-00-3, illustrated. $16.50.

CALIFOBIA (Colin White & Laurie Boucke)

A satirical romp through the madness and mayhem of Southern California. Test your sense of humor and irony, with LaLa Land exposed as never before. Sequel to "The UnDutchables." ISBN 0-9625006-4-X, 260 pages, illustrated. $12.25.

HEART & SOLE (David Stewart)

David Stewart's haunting account of his 1,600-mile walk from Gillette, Wyoming, to Nashville, Tennessee, in 1988, to realize a lifelong dream. Highly emotional reading, recommended for all ages. ISBN 0-9625006-6-6, 260 pages, illustrated. $12.50.

ROAD MANGLER DELUXE (Phil Kaufman)

The autobiography of Phil Kaufman, "executive nanny" to rock 'n roll/country music stars (from Frank Zappa to Emmylou Harris), Charles Manson confidante, and much more. ISBN 0-9625006-5-8, 328 pages, illustrated. $12.95.

STRIKE FOUR (Jeff Archer)

The sparkling, true story of one man's attempt to further the sport of baseball in Britain, France, Belgium, Germany and Holland. Rich in insight, humor and cultural expose. ISBN 0-9625006-7-4, 240 pages, illustrated. $12.50.

THE UNDUTCHABLES (Colin White & Laurie Boucke)

A satirical look at the Dutch nation. A must for anyone with Dutch connections. Repeated bestseller in Holland. ISBN 0-9625006-3-1, 280 pages, illustrated. $12.50.

TRICKLE TREAT (Laurie Boucke)

Infant toilet training taught from basics. A satisfying, environmentally sound method of toilet training. Start in infancy and finish when your baby walks. ISBN 0-9625006-2-3, 86 pages, illustrated. $7.50.

Our books can be obtained through your local bookstore or direct from the publisher at the price indicated plus $3.75 priority-mail shipping. CO residents add 7.4% sales tax. VISA, MC, AMEX and Discover cards accepted.

WHITE-BOUCKE PUBLISHING, PO Box 400, Lafayette, CO 80026, USA
Tel: (303) 604-0661, Fax: (303) 604-0662,
E-mail: 103531.2162@compuserve.com